The New Leader's Guide to Early Childhood Settings

T0386373

Learn how to effectively lead and make an impact in early childhood and primary school settings. *The New Leader's Guide to Early Childhood Settings* explores how to empower educators and caregivers, advocate for early intervention, promote culturally responsive teaching, and confront common fears and hurdles. Packed with helpful resources and strategies, chapters feature key tips about effective communication, leveraging technology, and questions for reflection. Practical and accessible, this engaging guidebook delivers quick, effective advice whether you're just starting out or are an experienced leader newly jumping into the early years.

Elaine Margarita Mendez is a Vice Principal in Newark Public Schools, USA. She has been an urban school educator for 17 years and has taught all grades K–5 as either a general education teacher, an ESL teacher, or a bilingual teacher.

Kenneth Kunz is the Director and Founder of For the Love of Literacy, LLC, and provides professional development to teachers in schools across the country. Ken is an author and literacy consultant and proudly serves as President of the International Literacy Association and on the Board of Directors of Little Free Library.

The New Leader's Guide to Early Childhood Settings

Making an Impact in PreK-3

Elaine Margarita Mendez and
Kenneth Kunz

Routledge
Taylor & Francis Group

NEW YORK AND LONDON

Cover image: © Shutterstock

First published 2023
by Routledge
605 Third Avenue, New York, NY 10158

and by Routledge
4 Park Square, Milton Park, Abingdon, Oxon, OX14 4RN

Routledge is an imprint of the Taylor & Francis Group, an informa business

© 2023 Elaine Margarita Mendez and Kenneth Kunz

Library of Congress Cataloging-in-Publication Data
Names: Mendez, Elaine Margarita, author. | Kunz, Kenneth, author.
Title: The new leader's guide to early childhood settings : making an impact in PreK-3 / Elaine Margarita Mendez and Kenneth Kunz.
Description: New York, NY: Routledge, 2023. | Series: Eye on education | Includes bibliographical references.
Identifiers: LCCN 2022019260 (print) | LCCN 2022019261 (ebook) | ISBN 9781032114057 (hardback) | ISBN 9781032110547 (paperback) | ISBN 9781003219767 (ebook)
Subjects: LCSH: Early childhood education–Administration. | Elementary school administration. | Educational leadership.
Classification: LCC LB2822.6 .M46 2023 (print) | LCC LB2822.6 (ebook) | DDC 372.12–dc23/eng/20220622
LC record available at https://lccn.loc.gov/2022019260
LC ebook record available at https://lccn.loc.gov/2022019261

ISBN: 9781032114057 (hbk)
ISBN: 9781032110547 (pbk)
ISBN: 9781003219767 (ebk)

DOI: 10.4324/9781003219767

Typeset in Optima
by Deanta Global Publishing Services, Chennai, India

Dedication

This work is for Juan, my best friend, and our three greatest accomplishments Nicholas, Olivia, and Penelope. I hope you all know that you will forever be my inspiration to continue to learn, grow, and be better than I was yesterday.

To teacher leaders, new leaders, current leaders, and aspiring leaders …

Remember, never a failure, always a lesson.

Peace and love,

Elaine Margarita

****

This book is dedicated to our existing and soon-to-be colleagues who will pave the way in early childhood for futures beyond imagining. To Elaine, who ran with an amazing idea and took it from "Can we?" to "Watch us!" May this book cultivate new leaders to seek out similar changemakers in the field as they grow, develop, and advocate on behalf of children everywhere.

Dr. Kenneth Kunz

Contents

Contents

About the Authors

Elaine Margarita Mendez is a proud instructional leader in Newark Public Schools. She received her bachelor's degree in Management and Sociology from Rutgers University–Newark, a master's degree in Teaching from Saint Peter's University, and a second master's degree in Instructional Leadership from Western Governor's University. Currently, Elaine is a Doctoral Candidate at Liberty University working toward the completion of a Doctor of Education degree in Curriculum and Instruction with an emphasis on Elementary Education. Over the course of her career, Elaine has served as a bilingual teacher, ESL teacher, general education teacher, and literacy coach. Elaine's passion for literacy, best teaching practices, teacher leadership, and mentoring have guided her educational interests and have inspired her to continue on the path of lifelong learning.

Dr. Kenneth Kunz is the Director and Founder of For the Love of Literacy, LLC. He holds a bachelor's degree in Elementary Education and English from Kean University and a master's degree in Reading Specialization and a doctorate in Teacher Leadership from Rutgers University. He has received recognition as an outstanding teacher through the New Jersey Governor's Teacher Recognition Program and was awarded the Edward Fry Endowed Fellowship in Literacy at Rutgers University in 2014. He currently serves as President of the International Literacy Association and leads on the Board of Directors for Little Free Library and NJ Literacy Association. He has presented professional development centered on literacy instruction in classrooms across New Jersey and at both state and national conferences and is co-author of *Breaking through the Language Arts Block: Organizing and Managing an Exemplary Literacy Day* and *Literacy Changemakers: Bringing the Joy of Reading and Writing into Focus for Students and Teachers*.

Acknowledgments

I would like to extend my gratitude and appreciation to my Professional Learning Network whom I lovingly refer to as my Twitter Family! Your suggestions, words of encouragement, guidance, and support have been instrumental in my leadership growth and development.

A special "THANK YOU" also goes to Ms. Annamaria Contella. In 2017 we embarked on our first teacher leadership journey together as instructional coaches. Our experiences learning, planning, and ultimately leading professional development and instructional coaching sessions gave birth to my passion for leading. Together, we learned to navigate our teacher leadership role. We cheered our successes and reflected on our mistakes. I am forever grateful for her guidance and support.

I also want to acknowledge the many wonderful leaders I have met in Newark Public Schools. Your commitment to our children is incredibly inspiring. I am proud to lead alongside each and every one of you. Thank you for helping me grow, but above all, thank you for believing in me.

With gratitude,

Elaine Margarita Mendez

Introduction

Whether you are a teacher, coach, vice principal, or principal, learning to navigate the world of early childhood settings, be mindful that effective leadership does not occur overnight. It is a process that requires some adjustment and navigating through learning curves. If you picked up this book, chances are that you frequently turn to books to find answers, seek new strategies, acquire new perspectives, and challenge your thinking. We wanted to write this book to share our perspectives and experiences in the hopes that it will help guide and support your transition into effective changemakers in early childhood and primary school settings. The chapters will provide you with thought-provoking questions, practical and easy to implement leadership tips, an equity perspective, and inspiration. We have fused our collective learned experiences with research-based practices and learning theories to provide you with an overview of what your journey will entail.

As lifelong learners who personify learning mindsets, we hope that you use this book to build a foundation and gain motivation to keep on growing and learning. While each chapter has embedded space for writing quick reflections, we encourage you to maintain a journal and jot down key takeaways and next steps to consider as you critically think and reflect on the readings.

The book is divided into three parts. Part I will provide you a glimpse into the world of early childhood. Theories of learning and human development are explored. Ways to foster learning environments that are driven by the concept of care and your role in the process are discussed. The section concludes with an exploration of social, emotional, and academic learning in early childhood settings. Part II shifts to a discussion on how early childhood learners are engaged and motivated to participate in the learning opportunities provided in schools and classrooms. We discuss effective leadership characteristics conducive to a positive and engaging learning environment. This portion of the book is full of suggestions to help you cultivate caring, positive, and student-centered learning environments. Part III is all about you, the leader. We define five leadership styles and suggest ways that will help you identify your own style of leading. We provide suggestions for leading with equity and suggest ways to practice self-care and embody a lifelong learning mindset.

Each chapter begins with a positive affirmation. These affirmations or mantras have been a constant in our work and our leadership journey. We are incredibly proud of this work and hope that it sheds light on who you are as a leader, changemaker, and champion for our youngest learners. The ultimate goal of this book is to help YOU realize that you CAN do amazing things in your school setting. If nothing else, we want you to remember that mistakes are a part of the process that should be perceived as opportunities to learn and to grow.

Part I: A Glimpse into the World of Early Childhood

Chapter 1: *The work I do really matters.*

Chapter 2: *I can positively impact students' lives.*

Chapter 3: *I feel joy when students receive the support they need.*

Part II: Understanding Teaching, Learning, Student Engagement, and Recognition in Early Childhood Settings

Chapter 4: *I can ignite a love for learning.*

Chapter 5: *I can design a learning agenda that builds students' background knowledge and passion for critical thinking.*

Chapter 6: *I feel accomplished when students are learning.*

Part III: Leading in Early Childhood Settings

Chapter 7: *I know my purpose.*

Chapter 8: *I am intentional about cultivating an inclusive culture.*

Chapter 9: *Mistakes are proof that I am trying.*

Chapter 10: *I welcome change and grow from experiences.*

We would like to hear from and engage with you. We are active members on social media and would love it if you joined our Professional Learning

Network. To keep the conversation going, connect with us via Twitter. We are looking forward to hearing your thoughts, suggestions, questions, or comments.

Peace and love …

Elaine Margarita Mendez
Twitter handle: @ElemCoach
Dr. Kenneth Kunz
Twitter handle: @DrKennethKunz

A Glimpse into the World of Early Childhood

Understanding Early Childhood and Primary School Settings

Positive Affirmation: The Work I Do Matters

We imagine that each day you walk into your office you do so ready to tackle whatever the day may bring. Sometimes, chaotic situations will arise and demand most of your attention, while other days may be full of joy or a combination of both. Whatever kind of day you face, we want you to know that the work you do matters. It matters to the eager children who come to school to learn and make new friends. It matters to the parents and caregivers who trust that their precious children are educated, cared for, and kept safe while under your care. It matters to the dedicated teachers and staff members who consistently give their **all** to deliver instructional content that meets the diverse social, emotional, and academic needs of the students within their classrooms.

Every day is full of new possibilities, challenges, and opportunities. As early childhood leaders, you have the heroic task of guiding, shaping, and ensuring that our youngest learners can effectively maneuver their way through the concept of schooling. Throughout your journey, remember that the work you do truly matters.

****

Evolving Learning and Human Development Theories

Early childhood and primary school settings are responsible for educating children between the ages of three and eight. In terms of schooling, this age

DOI: 10.4324/9781003219767-2

span translates to students in grades pre-kindergarten through third grade. This period sets the stage for all future learning experiences throughout a child's lifespan leading them into successful adulthood. Considering the impact of early childhood education upon a child's successful transition to adulthood, researchers have devoted time to exploring the stages of childhood development.

Thanks to the abundance of research on early childhood, learning, and human development, we have been able to identify that learning occurs in stages, that learning opportunities must be developmentally appropriate, and that children leverage their experiences to solidify knowledge. For these reasons, we felt it would be helpful to provide you with a brief overview of specific learning and human development theories that have helped shape early childhood and primary education. As you read the chapter, consider your school setting and the ways in which your leadership is focused on honoring how children learn best.

In *Literacy Development in the Early Years: Helping Children Read and Write*, Morrow (2015) explains: "Early childhood education is not a recent development. Since the 1700s, philosophers, theorists, psychologists, and educators have addressed appropriate educational practices for learning in early childhood" (p. 4). As we unpack some of the major influences/influencers of early childhood learning, consider using the "My Thought Tracker" template (Table 1.1) to stop and jot down important thoughts and ideas about how these theories have manifested themselves in your own early childhood experiences and how they might play a role in how you advocate for the needs of emergent/early learners.

While we see evidence of approaches dating back to the eighteenth and nineteenth centuries and philosophies of Rousseau (nature and curiosity), Pestalozzi (use of artifacts or "gifts" for learning), and Froebel (use of play), the twentieth and twenty-first centuries continue to evolve and

Table 1.1 My Thought Tracker

My Thought Tracker		
Learning and human development theory	Personal experiences, thoughts, or connections	What this means for leading in the early childhood environment
Behaviorism		
Cognitive development theory		

broaden our understanding of theories and practices for young learners. Consider some more notable names in the field of education:

- John Dewey: If you have ever experienced "circle time" or centers/workstations while in school, then you can relate to the progressive, child-centered ideas of Dewey.
- B.F. Skinner: Remember explicit instruction around letters and sounds when learning the English alphabet? If so, your imitation and association through conditioning led to your automatic response, which is aligned with how behaviorists view learning.
- Maria Montessori: Montessori schools believe in the use of manipulatives for learning and relying on the five senses.

Read on to find out what else you might consider as an early childhood leader. While this chapter is not an exhaustive list of practices and theories impacting young learners, you are likely beginning to see that decades of research have impacted, and continue to impact, our understanding of what works best for young learners.

Leadership tip: At the beginning of the chapter, the following affirmation launched our exploration: *The work I do matters*. Keep in mind that your work must involve unpacking research, theories, and evolving best practices. Set a goal for joining a professional organization to stay on top of the latest in your field. Avoid "We've always done it this way" ways of thinking, and build your early childhood network (hint: Some helpful links are shared at the end of this chapter).

Cognitive Development Theory

Another influential theory of learning derived from the work of Jean Piaget (1896–1980) is cognitive development theory. This theory suggests that changes in behavior or understanding result from children's interactions with the world around them. Piaget believed that children were actively involved in their cognitive development by leveraging their interactions to form new knowledge, build upon existing knowledge, or modify assumptions previously made (Piaget, 1926). Essentially, the cognitive development theory focuses on how individuals acquire knowledge (Schunk, 2020). Figure 1.1

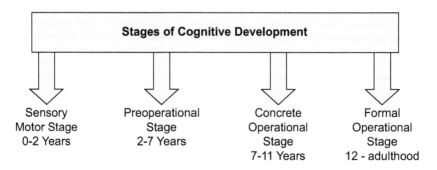

Figure 1.1 Graphic identifying Piaget's four *stages of cognitive development.*

identifies the four categories or stages of cognitive development. Children entering early childhood and primary school settings are between three and eight years old. Using the stages of development identified by Piaget, we understand that children in these educational settings are operating within the preoperational stage and transition toward the concrete operational stage as they enter third grade. During the preoperational stage, children dive into a period characterized by increased language development leading to a less egocentric view of the world and the realization that others may have opinions that differ from their own (Schunk, 2020). This development growth stage spans from two years to seven years old. Beginning at the age of seven, children transition to the concrete operational stage. It is during this stage that children begin to use their personal experiences, or schema, to understand the world around them.

Due partly to Piaget's contributions, we acknowledged that cognitive development does not occur in isolation. As children interact with their environment, they actively participate and grow through each stage of development. Different experiences, behaviors, and interactions culminate in creating a child's respective worldview. Therefore, early childhood and primary education settings need to provide children with developmentally appropriate learning opportunities and tasks. Embedding opportunities for exploration and hands-on activities help children construct and build upon their cognitive development (Schunk, 2020). As an early childhood leader, a clear understanding of the stages of cognitive development will assist you in ensuring that your teams are positively contributing to the creation of learning environments that foster children's cognitive development through engaging activities and promoting children's social interactions.

Multiple Intelligences Theory

The *Cambridge Dictionary* defines intelligence as "the ability to learn, understand, and make judgments or have opinions based on reason" (*Cambridge Dictionary*, 2021). Howard Gardner (1983) proposed that people do not just have one ability or way of learning; rather, people have many ways by which they could successfully learn. His multiple intelligences theory suggests that human beings can use the environment around them to continue to learn throughout their lifespan. Table 1.2 illustrates Gardner's eight multiple intelligences and their corresponding strengths. Early childhood curricula should be written in a way that promotes and cultivates the different intelligences that guide our youngest learners to develop a sense of confidence and love for learning. When we honor children's multiple intelligences, we cultivate inclusive learning environments where students generally thrive. The idea that children can encompass multiple intelligences is essential for early childhood educators and leaders alike.

In *Visible Learning*, Hattie (2008) cautions that multiple intelligences can often be difficult for educators to accurately assess. After analyzing 8 meta-analyses and 411 studies, Hattie suggests that instead of focusing on determining the learning styles of our young learners, we should aim to effectively (1) teach strategies for learning aligned with different ways of doing, and (2) monitor students' preferences for learning over making our own assumptions. Our takeaway is to think strategy and joy around the intelligences as opposed to spending energy matching "styles" to individual

Table 1.2 A Chart Identifying the Eight *Multiple Intelligences* as Identified by Howard Gardner

Eight Multiple Intelligences	Strengths
Verbal/linguistic	Writing, speaking, language skills
Logical/mathematical	Investigating and analyzing problems, mathematics
Musical/rhythmic	Movement, music, singing, dance
Visual/spatial	Visual and spatial strengths
Bodily/kinesthetic	Physical movement, good coordination, doers
Interpersonal	Ability to understand, communicate, relate to others
Intrapersonal	Self-awareness and self-reflection
Naturalistic	Interested in science, outdoors, plants, people

learners. More important is providing access to different ways for engagement and understanding.

Leadership tip: Assess how often/when opportunities for learning around the eight multiple intelligences are present in the classroom learning environments in your school community. Emphasize that strategy and joy are collectively more effective than simply trying to label learners with specific styles for learning.

Psychosocial Theory

Another theory of learning that has impacted early childhood education is based on the work of Erik Erikson (1902–1994). Erikson (1963) focused on human psychosocial growth and development. Table 1.3 depicts these eight stages of growth and development. Each stage highlights a psychosocial struggle requiring both internal regulation and external support to guide human beings to successfully make adaptations that will lead them toward achieving the desired outcomes and successfully moving on to the next stage of psychosocial development (Erikson, 1963).

Based on Erikson's (1963) work, we could identify the developmental stages for our early childhood and primary school aged learning group of students as being in the initiative v. guilt (3–5 years old) and industry v. inferiority (6–11 years old) stages. During these stages, students should begin to take initiative, explore, make friends, feel good about themselves, and ultimately develop a sense of confidence that will propel them toward continued psychosocial growth and development. As an early childhood leader,

Table 1.3 A Chart Identifying the Eight *Stages and Outcomes of Psychosocial Development*

Psychosocial Stage	Outcomes
Basic trust v. mistrust (birth–1 year old)	Hope
Autonomy v. shame and doubt (2 years old)	Will
Initiative v. guilt (3–5 years old)	**Purpose**
Industry v. inferiority (6–11 years old)	**Confidence**
Identity v. role diffusion (12–18 years old)	Fidelity
Intimacy v. isolation (young adulthood)	Love
Generative v. stagnation (adult–middle years)	Care
Ego integrity v. despair (older years)	Wisdom

understanding these stages will enable you to assess your program fully and identify how the learning environment you help cultivate can support children's psychosocial growth and development.

Sociocultural Theory

Developmental psychologist Lev Vygotsky (1896–1934) formulated the sociocultural theory. His findings are founded upon ideas that children's learning experiences are influenced by their home culture, spoken language, and family life. Part of his beliefs also included the notion that those influences were responsible for developing students' self-identities. Perhaps the greatest contribution resulting from the sociocultural theory was the identification of the zone of proximal development. Vygotsky defined the zone of proximal development as the difference between what children could do on their own versus what they could achieve with the support of others (Schunk, 2020). Aside from leading us to identify social interactions as being crucial to learning, the sociocultural theory helped construct how many early childhood and primary education settings currently operate.

Maslow's Hierarchy of Needs

Although it is not a learning theory per se, we felt it was pertinent to include a brief discussion based on Maslow's hierarchy of needs as this body of research has important implications related to early childhood and primary settings. Abraham Maslow (1908–1970) was a psychologist who believed that "students' developmental levels vary according to how well their biological and psychological needs have been satisfied" (Parkay et al., 2014). Maslow's hierarchy of needs is a motivation theory that suggests human actions and behaviors strive to meet or satisfy needs (Schunk, 2020). On the hierarchy of needs Figure 1.2, typically depicted as a pyramid, Maslow identified five basic needs: physiological, safety, belongingness, esteem, and self-actualization. The basic needs found at the lower portion of the pyramid must be met or satisfied before students can scale up the pyramid of needs and ultimately reach self-actualization, the highest on the pyramid.

Understanding Maslow's hierarchy of needs can have significant implications for early childhood and primary school settings. Knowing our

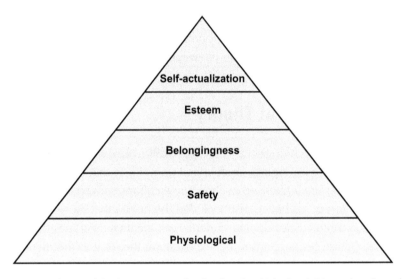

Figure 1.2 The graphic demonstrates the five levels of *Maslow's hierarchy of needs*.

children and their needs can help school leaders plan and lead initiatives that result in schools that leverage resources to ensure students' needs are met. To be quite clear, if our youngest learners are coming to us hungry, scared, and feeling isolated, there is an excellent chance that their motivation to want to engage in learning opportunities will be nonexistent.

Integrated Systems of Student Support

Our description of Maslow's hierarchy of needs is an excellent segue to a brief discussion on the importance of developing and fostering an integrated system of support to help solidify your efforts and results as an early childhood and primary school leader. An integrated system of student support is "a strategy for promoting students' academic success by securing and coordinating supports that target academic and non-academic barriers to achievement to promote improved student outcomes" (Wasser Gish, 2019).

We previously shared the notion that when our youngest learners come to school hungry, feeling unsafe, worried, etc., their motivation to engage in learning may be lacking. One way to ensure that basic needs, as described by Maslow's hierarchy of needs, are met is by developing integrated student support systems. These systems require coordination, collaboration, and frequent communication between the parties involved. These parties may include but are not limited to school leaders, teacher teams, school social workers, school counselors, outside agencies, parents, parent liaisons or parent coordinators, nurses, and community partners like the Boys and Girls Club or Big Brother Big Sister. Research on integrated student support systems has yielded positive impacts on increased student attendance, improved student engagement, higher academic achievement, reduced high school dropout rates, and better social and emotional outcomes (Wasser Gish, 2019).

By establishing and nurturing a practical integrated system of student support, you will essentially demonstrate to students, their families, and the school community that your school is not a lonesome entity. Instead, you will be promoting the notion that it takes a village to successfully educate a child. Through these different partnerships, you will ultimately enhance your schools' ability to meet the varying needs of the diverse children under your care and guide them one step closer toward being successful students and adults.

Children's Rights as Learners

In collaboration with several different countries, the United Nations Children's Fund (UNICEF) generated the Convention of the Rights of the Child (CRC) to ensure and promote an awareness of children's rights. The following language can be found on UNICEF's site and speaks to the purpose and goals of the convention:

> The Convention on the Rights of the Child is an international treaty that recognizes the human rights of children, defined as persons up to the age of 18 years. The Convention establishes in international law that States Parties must ensure that all children – without discrimination in any form – benefit from special protection measures and assistance; have access to services such as education and health care; can develop their personalities, abilities, and talents to the fullest potential; grow up in an environment of happiness, love, and understanding; and are informed about and participate in, achieving their rights in an accessible and active manner.
>
> (Convention on the Rights of the Child, 1989)

While there are a total of 54 Articles encompassing the Convention on the Rights of the Child, for this text, we want to bring awareness to Articles 28 through 31 as they specifically address children's rights in learning and instructional settings.

- **Article 28** of the CRC provides guidance on children's rights to education. It dictates that children have the right to a free, equal opportunity to a primary education. This right also requires frequent encouragement to continue pursuing higher education with opportunities for children to choose from vocational or more traditional secondary learning environments.

- **Article 29** explores the aims of education. It establishes the notion that education should help form the whole child. Thus, the objective of education is for children to understand how the world works, learn to interact with others, develop a sense of self, and grow into positive and contributing members of society.

- **Article 30** relates to minority culture, language, and religion. This article depicts children's rights to leverage their native language and culture as they learn regardless of the dominant language.

- **Article 31** explores children's rights to play, rest, and engage in culture and arts activities.

As an early childhood primary school leader, it is imperative to lead educational programs grounded upon these ideals and consistently work to ensure that children engage in learning environments that promote their growth and development through an academic lens as well as a social and emotional lens.

What Does Developmentally Appropriate Mean?

After reading through the brief descriptions of learning theories that impact early childhood and primary schools, you may be wondering how to define developmentally appropriate as it relates to your school setting. Our favorite definition of this concept comes from the National Association for the Education of Young Children (NAEYC). The NAEYC (2021) defines a developmentally appropriate practice as relating to strategies that optimize children's learning through a culturally, linguistically, and ability-appropriate, strength-based, play-based approach to both joyful and engaged learning. This definition considers the importance of creating a learning environment that focuses not only on what children need to learn but doing so with the understanding that learning must consider their culture, linguistic abilities, and strengths. Developmentally appropriate learning environments allow children to gain confidence, find their voice, and ask questions as they engage in learning.

Armed with this definition, an understanding of children's rights, and developmental theories of learning you can now begin to formulate a student-centered or child-centered approach to leading a developmentally appropriate early childhood or primary school setting where children are free to express themselves, ask questions about things they are curious about, play, join in conversations, and begin to understand their place in the world.

Eye on equity: To effectively lead learning environments that acknowledge students' developmental needs on both the academic and social-emotional spectrum you must develop an equity mindset. An equity mindset will help you as you lead your teachers, grade-level teams, and staff members to welcome and acknowledge students just as they are; thus, creating opportunities for all students to embrace their lived experiences while acquiring the knowledge to continue to grow and thrive in school. Equity mindsets enhance learning for all students.

Final Thoughts

Early childhood and primary school settings are responsible for educating students between three to eight years old. This age span also encompasses grade levels pre-kindergarten to third. There are vast differences in children's learning and development during this timeframe. Learning and development theories have guided our understanding of these differences. Piaget identified four stages of cognitive development. Gardner developed the idea that there are multiple intelligences and that children learn in different modalities. Erikson shed light on how children experience growth and development through the identification of eight psychosocial stages of development. Vygotsky identified the zone of proximal development and helped shed light on how social interactions correlate to learning. Maslow developed a hierarchy demonstrating that children must have their basic needs met before they can devote their focus to learning.

Our discussion also included the importance of establishing a solid integrated system of student support whereby schools collaborate and partner with parents, community members, and other partners to ensure that schools can effectively meet student needs and lead students to success.

Finally, we discussed the idea that children are protected and have rights as established by the Convention on Children's Rights. We focused on children's rights to an education and their right to play, relax, and engage in arts activities. These ideas have implications for your work as an early childhood leader. It is imperative that you lead teachers in cultivating developmentally appropriate learning environments that result in children who prosper academically, socially, and emotionally.

Our Favorite Chapter Resource Links
- UNICEF: Convention on the Rights of the Child Website https://www.unicef .org/child-rights-convention
- Convention on the Rights of the Child Infographic https://childhub.org/en
- Center for Promise: America's Promise Alliance: Americaspromise.org
- National Association for the Education of Young Children: https://www.naeyc .org

---

Chapter 1: Reflection Questions

- What implications do learning theories have for early childhood learners?
- How am I helping my teams enhance learning and developing opportunities for students?
- What systems of student support do I have in place?
- How do I know that the needs of my students are considered by my staff?

Chapter 1: Understanding Early Childhood and Primary School Settings

Leadership Action Spotlight

Identify three takeaways from Chapter 1.

_____

_____

_____

Write down two ideas that you would like to implement in your current role.

OR for aspiring leaders

Write down two ideas that you would consider implementing in the future.

_____

_____

_____

Identify one lingering question or area you would like to explore further.

_____

_____

_____

Personal reflection, thoughts, comments, concerns, ideas:

_____

_____

_____

_____

_____

2 | Cultivating a Caring and Responsive Learning Environment

Positive Affirmation: I Can Positively Impact Students' Lives

Let your daily interactions be rewarding and productive. As the leader of your school, you will set the tone for the culture of your building. Establishing a caring and responsive culture will help in your quest to impact the lives of the students you serve. Don't dwell on things that may not go as planned. Instead, use those experiences to reflect on how to continue to positively impact your students.

****

What Does the Research Say about Caring?

In Chapter 1, we briefly introduced you to Maslow's hierarchy of needs. We discussed the idea that to reach the stage of self-actualization, or a strong desire to succeed, children must have their basic needs met (Schunk, 2020). These basic needs may include but are not limited to feeling safe, cared for, loved, and having food to eat when hungry.

The reality is that many of our students may not have these basic needs met resulting in a lack of focus in school. For instance, food insecurity has continued to plague students living in low-income households. A study conducted by Gallegos et al. (2021) found that there is a strong positive correlation between food insecurity and academic, cognitive outcomes, as well as externalizing behaviors in students. The researchers further discussed that food insecurity creates a sense of anxiety in children which limits their ability to focus.

DOI: 10.4324/9781003219767-3

In our teaching and leading journey, we have identified feeling cared for as the one feeling that helps classrooms and schools thrive. These feelings are supported by researchers like Nel Noddings (2013) who asserts that this is both a necessity in education and a moral responsibility. Noddings believes that these principles also lead us to be more ethical decision-makers. To accomplish this, we must prioritize (1) leading by example, (2) fostering open dialogue and multiple opportunities for communication, (3) developing caring and empathetic learners, and (4) confirming the best in others (Noddings, 2013).

Leadership tip: Start a "Leadership Action Book Club" to focus on the concept of caring in education. While the examples in this chapter provide a launch point for exploring this topic, choose a book club text to ground your discussions. Encourage members of the book club to bring their own research to the conversation.

When our students feel that their teachers, vice principals, and principals genuinely care for them, they are more likely to go to school ready to learn and engage with their peers. Caring also encompasses the act of being responsive to the needs of our students. This includes being responsive to their linguistic, developmental, academic, social, and emotional needs. As early childhood leaders, you must be aware of these needs. In doing so, you will be paving the way toward creating a caring and responsive learning environment where students can grow and learn through developmentally appropriate practices.

Your Role in Cultivating a Caring and Responsive Environment

How can you, as an early childhood leader, attempt to ensure that all your students' needs are met? At this point, you are probably thinking … "I am just one person. There's just no way." Please stop … breathe … and remember: You are the leader! It is your mission to facilitate an environment that supports the developmental and social emotional growth of our children. Refer to Chapter 1 and our discussion of integrating a system of student supports and recall that you are NOT alone! You have an entire staff consisting of certified, capable, and caring educators, nurturing school counselors, social workers, nurses, and a community to call upon.

Effective instructional leaders forge positive and fruitful relationships that facilitate the tremendous amount of work necessary to adequately lead schools. Relationships are at the core of cultivating caring and responsive learning environments. Say it again and write this mantra down in your planner: *I am not alone! I am the instructional leader of a capable team.* Learn to leverage your teams and cultivate the caring and responsive learning environment that all children need. It all starts with YOU!

As you consider how to get initiatives off the ground, how to support your instructional teams, how to guide your non-instructional staff, and how to engage your parents and community partners, realize that you must be active and present. Your visibility is crucial to cultivating a caring and responsive environment. One important aspect of your instructional leadership role is recognizing your teachers and staff members. It is important for you to develop positive relationships with your teams. This is achieved through active listening and by acknowledging the needs of the adults in your building. Ensure that your teams are aware of your commitment to the success of the school. Promote the notion that the overall success of your learning environment requires a collective effort in promoting the vision and mission of the school. Consider the social, emotional, and professional needs of your staff. Teora Brooks-Summers, a caring school leader in an urban school district, shares weekly check-in emails with her instructional teams. She provides them with positive affirmations, articles on relevant professional development opportunities, and resources for staff to engage in self-reflection. Through her actions, Ms. Brooks-Summers has established herself as an instructional leader who genuinely cares for the well-being of her staff.

Acknowledging other stakeholders is crucial as well. Greet parents and caretakers as they drop off their children at school each morning. They need to see you! Visibility in the playground, a simple "good morning" or "hello," can help parents feel at ease when dropping off their babies at school. It is also the first step in establishing a positive home-to-school connection.

Your students need to see you too. Conduct "Pop Up" visits to different classrooms each day to say "hello" and to check in on the social, emotional, and academic needs of the children. Stop by the playground during recess time and interact with them. Ask about their day and encourage them to share. Be visible during dismissal time, and let students know that you cannot wait to see them again. A high five (or fist bump), a smile and words of encouragement, or other agreed upon form of salutation or greeting, can go a long way in forming relationships and giving you the visibility needed to create a caring and responsive learning environment.

Leadership tip: If you lead in an environment with many scholars, use alliteration to help remember students' names. Shalonda Archibald, a literacy changemaker in New Jersey, asks students to think about the initial sounds of their first names. She then uses descriptive words to match the sounds. Before long, she is able to recognize "Grateful Gerard" or "Magnificent Monaja" during her travels throughout the school building and in the hallways.

It is easy to get inundated with paperwork, calls, and meetings leading you to overlook an opportunity to engage with students. Therefore, aim to be intentional about making these experiences happen. Create a schedule and block out time for your daily "Pop Up Visits" and interactions. Table 2.1 is an example of how you may want to structure your day to ensure you visit classrooms and interact with students throughout the day. We all know that things happen, and schedules could be interrupted; however, when you intentionally plan your visits and interactions, you have a greater chance of sticking to your plans and building consistent visibility.

Thinking outside the box can also help you establish a caring and responsive learning environment. For example, morning announcements are one way to start the day off on the right foot, so to speak. Why not involve your students in the act? Have a rotating schedule where you allow students to share something special, recite the flag salute, or read an important announcement. You might also feature a daily affirmation and student

Table 2.1 Sample Weekly Schedule Showing Intentional Interactions with Students

Time	Monday	Tuesday	Wednesday	Thursday	Friday
8:00 AM	Welcome/ greet PK students	Welcome/greet kindergarten students	Welcome/ greet first graders	Welcome/ greet second graders	Welcome/ greet third graders
9:00 AM					
10:00 AM	Pop Up Visits	Pop Up Visits	Pop Up Visits	Pop Up Visits	Pop Up Visits
11:00–1:00 Lunches	Make time to interact with students during their lunch/recess time.				
1:00 PM					
2:00 PM					
3:00 PM	Be visible during dismissal. Wave and smile as your students leave for the day.				

shout outs for adhering to your school's core values during this time. Your older students will often feel honored to complete the task, and the younger ones will dream about the day in which they too will get the chance to read an announcement. In our experiences, we have seen many students practicing their fluency for days to sound "just right" when delivering their message to the school community.

Another way through which you could be visible and continue to nurture responsive and caring environments is through videos. During weeks where you know your schedule is going to be tight because of assessments, professional development, or the many other administrative tasks you will undoubtedly handle, you can record quick two-to-three-minute video clips for your students to watch. One of our favorite website applications for this very purpose is Flipgrid (www.flipgrid.com). Flipgrid is a child-friendly, video-making, web-based application. You can create short video clips, and students can respond to your clips in class or at home. Overall, your role in cultivating caring and responsive classroom environments is instrumental as you are the face of your school.

Leadership tip: In *All Learning Is Social and Emotional: Helping Students Develop Essential Skills for the Classroom and Beyond* (2019), Fisher, Frey, and Smith remind us that the social and emotional curriculum does not need to be "hidden." As a leader, you can gather your stakeholders to draft what is at the core of your school's values. Consider including "caring" as one of your values!

Setting the Learning Environment

Imagine that you just walked by your favorite store. Think about that feeling you get deep down in your heart. Part of you wants to go running in just to check out how things are or to see if there is anything new and exciting. We'd like to think that schools and classroom settings should evoke the same feelings for our young learners. A child's school and in particular the classroom should be a place that draws attention. As the leader of the building, you must ensure that your school emits this type of captivating feeling.

Remember that children in early childhood and primary schools need to be guided by developmentally appropriate practices, strategies, and resources. This applies to the learning environment too. When you walk into an early childhood and primary school, the atmosphere should be inviting. There should be colorful signs, posters, and child-centered language indicating that this is THE place to learn, grow, and develop. Evidence of children's work should not be hidden but proudly displayed fostering a sense of pride and acceptance. Chairs and desks should be height appropriate. The arrangement of the classroom must be spacious and conducive to different interests. Books should be visibly displayed in book bins and shelves, manipulatives ought to be visible, crayons and writing tools should be available as well. In Chapter 6, we provide more tips for learning environments specific to literacy and promoting a joy around growing as readers and writers.

How can you ensure that the learning environment is set for optimized learning? One suggestion is to conduct walkthroughs and ensure that classrooms have all the necessary resources, materials, and supplies to create a warm and welcoming atmosphere that elicits children's natural curiosity. Ask your teacher teams to identify supplies needed. Encourage the writing of grants if funds are lacking. One of our favorite grant resources is Donorschoose.org. Through this site, teachers can write grants based on what they need. In return, virtual donors can choose to fund a portion of the teachers' grant requests. The grant stays open until it is fully funded. At the same time, we believe that administrators need to communicate needs in this area when drafting, reviewing, and confirming school budgets.

Leveraging Your Staff

Your building staff consists of a plethora of different individuals with different responsibilities and skill sets. Once again, to impact student outcomes, you must establish relationships with your staff. Get to know their strengths, the things they enjoy, and be empathetic to their respective needs. Use your newfound knowledge to facilitate the making of magic in your buildings. This creation of magic in schools calls for everyone to understand, be a part of, and work toward the end goal: Improving student outcomes. Use both your school's mission and vision statements to generate a shared responsibility. Invite teachers to identify problems of practice and encourage them to also develop and implement strategies that could help mitigate said problems. When educators work together, schools become hubs for opportunities not just for our students but also for teachers, staff members, and school leadership.

Eliciting teacher and staff input is the first step in identifying what can be improved upon in your quest to cultivate a caring and responsive learning environment. You may want to host an open forum discussion whereby you engage staff members in targeted discussions around school-related topics and student needs. If the idea of an open forum seems terrifying, employ the use of surveys through Google Forms or Survey Monkey. This type of information collection will prompt teachers and staff to anonymously share their perception of the school's strengths and weaknesses, thus allowing you to gather data that will help you make informed decisions. Ultimately, you want your staff to feel empowered about sharing both their concerns and suggestions for improvement with you as the building leader. Teachers and staff members who express their concerns are often instrumental in creating growth opportunities for schools.

In the examples included below, we hope you can identify how the strength of teachers and staff members could be utilized to help develop a caring and responsive environment where everyone feels respected, included, and essential.

Example 1: Social and Emotional Care

Ms. Ferreira, a School Counselor, and Ms. Funcia, a School Social Worker, approached their administrative leader about the need for a functional student-centered social and emotional room. They advocated for a physical location where students could go to calm down and regulate their emotions. The pair conducted research on social and emotional learning and its impact on academics. They spent countless hours engrossed in curating resources to make the room inviting, warm, and student-friendly. Their vision included flexible seating, colorful rugs, wall décor, and high-interest children's books. After reviewing their request, school leaders were able to facilitate their vision and fund the purchase of the items necessary to get started. These staff members' motivation was high, and their intentions were grounded on caring for students and being responsive to their needs. The room itself was just a room, but the love, time, and effort spent in transforming it into a calming zone generated excitement and school-wide support for the social and emotional well-being of students.

Example 2: Care and Support for English Learners

Ms. Machado and Ms. Ribeiro noticed an increased number of English language learners (ELLs) enrolling in school. These teachers understood the struggles faced by their growing population of newcomers (students new to the linguistic demands of English as a second language, while at the same time becoming familiar with a new school) and realized that these students could benefit from participating in an ELL Club where they could use the time to speak freely, ask questions, connect with their peers, and begin to take the linguistic risks necessary to learn to speak a different language. After a discussion with their instructional leadership team, the teachers were given the lead to start a Language Development Before and After School Program. They worked together to identify the newcomers, reached out to their respective teachers, contacted parents, and began to engage students practicing and developing listening and speaking skills that would eventually transfer into the classroom. This example is evidence that teachers have a great deal of knowledge and experience with identifying and defining what students need to be successful. It is also evidence of how leaders can utilize teachers' strengths and interests to cultivate caring and responsive learning environments in schools.

Example 3: Care and Support for All Students

We all know that school attendance is crucial to student success. When students are in school, they are being exposed to and engaged in comprehending, manipulating, and synthesizing information that will result in their future academic success. As such, we must recognize when students show up ready to learn. Celebrating student attendance can be a high motivator for students to show up daily. Ms. Taisha Miranda, Attendance Counselor, and Ms. Martha Abraham, Paraprofessional, understood the importance of celebrating students who showed up each day. To demonstrate appreciation to students' commitment to attend school daily, these two caring school professionals sprang into action. They coordinated and facilitated a red-carpet perfect attendance soiree for every student who had achieved perfect attendance during a marking period. The event included a pizza lunch, certificates, and teachers and staff as cheerleaders. As the children walked down the red carpet, they were beaming with happiness and grinning from ear to ear. This is an example of staff members who understand their moral responsibility to help generate caring and responsive learning environments for all students.

Leadership tip: Think about your students' needs. Host a brainstorming session with your teachers or grade-level teams and find ways in which you could work as a team to help mitigate those needs. You can also host a meeting or conduct a survey to find out what your teachers are passionate about. Think about how you could help them bring visions to life. In the end, both strategies will help you cultivate a caring and responsive learning environment.

It's All in the Design: Contexts for Learning (Hybrid, Virtual, Brick-and-Mortar)

Learning environments have changed since the original single-room schoolhouse from the past. Technological advancements have generated different opportunities for learning. Computers and the Internet have allowed for information to be shared among different individuals helping to promote ideas and spearhead movements. Most recently, the emergence of the COVID-19 virus led to a global pandemic resulting in the need for leaders to redefine the concepts of traditional classrooms. We saw students move from brick-and-mortar learning environments to virtual remote learning zones, eventually leading to the creation of a hybrid model consisting of a mix of both in-person and virtual/remote learning opportunities. Regardless of the context in which our early childhood students learn, you must ensure that the learning environment is child-centered and conducive to the developmental needs of the students. Table 2.2 suggests different resources, including those with "look fors" to ensure that virtual and hybrid learning environments still adhere to being developmentally appropriate and are structured in a way that supports caring and responsive practices.

Empowering Parents and Caregivers

Parents and caregivers are an integral part of the home and school connection. It is imperative that leaders maintain open lines of communication with parents. This could be facilitated through monthly newsletters posted

Table 2.2 Suggested Resources for Unpacking the Early Childhood Learning Environment

Learning Environment		
Brick-and-Mortar	Virtual	Hybrid
• NAEYC Classroom Observation Tool (https://www.naeyc.org /sites/default/files/ wysiwyg/user-72/ co_sv_itpks_-_2019 .pdf)	• *The Distance Learning Playbook, Grades K-12* (2021) by Fisher, Frey, and Hattie • *The Quick Guide to Simultaneous, Hybrid, and Blended Learning* (2021) by Fisher, Frey, Almarode, and Henderson-Rosser Time Spent in Virtual/Hybrid Contexts: According to the National Board for Professional Teaching Standards (https://www.nbpts.org/), elementary school-aged children can spend up to 1–2 hours a day on virtual instruction. Knowing that virtual learning was never meant to be a 6–7 hour live (synchronous) day, think about what your school can do to accommodate on-demand (asynchronous) learning opportunities. Use the resources above to help in developing those opportunities.	

on your school website or through frequent updates on your school's social media accounts. Many leaders shy away from the use of social media as they may perceive it to be invasive, time consuming, or intimidating. However, school accounts on social media platforms such as Twitter, Instagram, and Facebook could serve as hubs for information distribution facilitating the ease and flow of communication for parents and caregivers. Effective communication has the potential to increase parental engagement in schools. Like being visible on the playground and in classrooms, enacting the flow of information through social media will give you visibility outside of the school building, thus increasing your reach in ensuring that parents too feel the caring and responsive environment that you are cultivating for their children. Use social media to tell your school's story. Showcase the amazing things your teacher teams are doing along with the incredible work that students are producing. Social media can be a very valuable tool for you to spread the magic you are cultivating in school.

Another way through which leaders could empower parents and caregivers is by making them a part of the narrative. You cannot assume that parents and caregivers are familiar with the developmental, academic, social, and emotional needs of their children. Creating information sessions, workshops, and parent academies are some of the ways that school districts are actively engaging parents and caregivers. The purpose is to equip them with strategies, skills, and resources that will empower them and help them support their children while at home.

Your efforts in creating a welcoming, relaxed, and respectful environment for parents and caregivers can further increase your ability to generate a caring and responsive culture for all. When planning for parent workshops, be mindful of the times. We suggest alternating different meeting times to allow for parents to participate either in the morning, afternoon, or evening. You should also consider including weekend sessions as engagement opportunities for parents who work Monday through Friday. Lastly, given the increased use of technology, aim to include virtual sessions as well. Enable the recording of these sessions and create a video library hub that parents and caregivers could reference throughout the year.

Eye on equity: When thinking about opportunities for parent and caregiver engagement in your school, consider viewing participation through an equity lens. Reflect on the following questions: Is your school providing different days and times for parents to engage with the school? Are teachers and staff available to aid with translation? Are you utilizing different platforms to distribute information? Is the information provided in different languages? Have you generated a welcoming environment where parents feel empowered to ask questions and engage in different opportunities? Remember, a school does not exist in isolation.

Final Thoughts

This chapter focused on providing you with strategies to help cultivate a caring and responsive early childhood and primary learning environment. As an early childhood instructional leader, you are the face of your building. You must make a conscious effort to include the input of your teachers, staff members, parents, and caregivers. Allow them to critically review the day-to-day operations of the school, assess the needs of the building, and generate ideas to improve such. Empowering educators to act and effectuate change can help transform a school building and cultivate learning environments that are responsive to students' needs. By acknowledging the crucial role parents and caregivers play in students' education you will also help solidify another layer that is characteristic of positive and caring school cultures. Ensure that parents and caregivers have a voice in the decision-making process. Allow for the creation of opportunities for all parents to engage by allowing different times for school-related meetings and gatherings. Allowing for different times and methods to engage can help increase and enhance your home and school connections.

Our Favorite Chapter Resource Links
- Donorschoose.org
- Flipgrid.com
- Instagram.com
- Twitter.com
- Facebook.com
- YouTube.com

Chapter 2: Reflection Questions

- How will you make your mark in your school?
- How will you show your students that you care?
- How will you demonstrate care to teachers and staff?
- What strategies will help you develop a caring and responsive learning environment?

Chapter 2: Cultivating a Caring and Responsive Learning Environment

Leadership Action Spotlight

Identify three takeaways from Chapter 2.

Write down two ideas that you would like to implement in your current role.

OR for aspiring leaders

Write down two ideas that you would consider implementing in the future.

_____

_____

_____

Identify one lingering question or area you would like to explore further.

_____

_____

_____

Personal reflection, thoughts, comments, concerns, ideas:

_____

_____

_____

_____

_____

Promoting Students' Social, Emotional, and Academic Growth

Positive Affirmation: I Feel Joy When Students Receive the Support They Need

Joy is having great feelings of happiness. In early childhood and primary school settings, joy is the driving force of learning. Students genuinely love exploring new topics, learning new vocabulary, and collaborating with peers. School is full of wonderful experiences and incredible opportunities. As the leader, you help lead the efforts that allow joy to be at the center of it all. YOU set the tone for happiness to thrive.

Developmental Milestones in the Early Childhood Setting

Children's stages of development include specific milestones in the following four domains: Cognitive, physical, communication and speech, and the social and emotional domain. These milestones allow school leaders, teachers, and caregivers to identify how children are developing. It is important to familiarize yourself with these developmental milestones as understanding what your students should know and be able to do will give you an advantage in identifying ways to support your teachers and grade level teams as they try to meet the needs of the children in their classrooms. Below, we have included a brief description of the four domains.

Cognitive: The cognitive domain is characterized by thinking, memory, learning, and children's abilities to make sense of the world around

DOI: 10.4324/9781003219767-4

them. This includes increased vocabulary and the development of likes and interests.

Physical: The physical domain includes children's mobility and dexterity. The physical domain also includes the ability to correctly hold a pencil, color, draw, eat, and do things independently.

Communication and speech: The communication and speech domain relates to how children can learn and manipulate language. They can use new vocabulary words and are able to express themselves with more complex sentences.

Social and emotional domain: This domain is characterized by children's ability to make friends and regulate their emotions.

It is important for you to understand the developmental milestones that children in early and primary school settings should be exhibiting. Equipped with this knowledge, you will be able to support your teachers, grade level teams, and staff to make decisions that will help students succeed.

Understanding Multi-Tiered Systems of Support

While school is an incredible learning adventure, it does not mean that all students have an easy time learning. In Chapter 1, we discussed evolving learning and human development theories. We positioned learning as the process by which students begin to make sense of the world around them through their experiences coupled with the acquisition of new knowledge, skills, and behaviors. What happens when students have difficulty comprehending new ideas? In the case of English learners, what happens when students do not possess the content-specific vocabulary to effectively comprehend instruction? What if students lack the basic foundational skills? What if they have learning delays? There are so many situations that can impact student achievement. As an instructional leader, you must familiarize yourself with such situations and begin to think of ways, strategies, and ideas you could implement to help students meet their respective developmental milestones.

Multi-tiered systems of support were established to help facilitate student achievement by ensuring that students are provided with supplemental, differentiated, tailored instruction. Tiered systems of support are not just for academics. Students who struggle with meeting behavior expectations can also benefit from the implementation of a behavior tiered system of support. Typically, tiered systems of support are depicted as a pyramid. At the bottom, the wider part of the pyramid is Tier 1. Tier 1 consists of the core programs, curriculum, and content that students need to learn in their respective grade levels. Toward the middle part of the pyramid, you will find Tier 2. Tier 2 is made up of targeted instruction or supplemental support that allows students to obtain further instruction in small groups. Finally, at the top of the pyramid sits Tier 3 made up of intensive instructional supports that are provided to students who demonstrate great need. The students receiving Tier 3 instruction are aggressively monitored to ensure progress. An effective multi-tiered system of support will help struggling learners succeed in either academics or behaviors.

Leadership tip: In many schools, tiered systems of support follow a Response to Intervention (RTI) Model. While this is not always the case, it is important for leaders to familiarize themselves with different approaches to tiered systems of support. It is also crucial not to "assign" tiers to individuals in a school community. The tiers are designed to promote intentionality around meeting students' needs. At the same time, the frequency of intervention and services increases as students move up the tiers. It is also important to understand that Tier 3 is not synonymous with special education or special services. A helpful resource among many in this area is *RTI from All Sides: What Every Teacher Needs to Know* (2009) by Mary Howard.

What Does Tiered Support Look Like in the Core Subjects of English Language Arts (ELA) and Math?

Tiered support is a good teaching practice, and one that can be utilized to be impactful in both language arts and mathematics classrooms. This practice allows teachers to give students the academic support they need to understand the content. Typically, in both mathematics and literacy classes, teachers begin instruction by conducting whole group instruction to provide students with an overview of the topic, skill, or strategy of the day. The teacher observes and focuses on student inquiries, interactions with peers, and responses to independent work activities. Based on these observations, teachers identify which students may need additional support. This support is then provided via small group instruction. In literacy, teachers often conduct guided reading, strategy groupings, or reading conferences. Similarly, in mathematics teachers conduct guided math, strategy groupings, and skill interventions. These groupings are fluid and will change as students master concepts and skills. Actively monitoring student progress is key to ensuring the supports are serving their purpose.

Another way to identify struggling students in either math or literacy is through assessments. Whether you are utilizing formative or summative assessments, the data obtained can help you guide your grade-level teams' instructional decisions. Advocating for the grouping of students based on areas of strengths or weaknesses is one way for you to leverage data to facilitate instruction and planning. Your teachers will be able to extend additional scaffolding and support in areas of deficiencies while also providing opportunities for students to expand their learning. In early childhood and primary classrooms, centers are often utilized to allow students the opportunity to review previously learned skills, practice new skills, and attempt to try new skills through activities that expand upon their learning. Give your teachers time to collaborate, plan, and create centers that support and enhance learning.

What Does Tiered Behavior Support Look Like?

In addition to academic support, some students may also benefit from the implementation of behavioral support. Establishing a tiered behavior support system in early childhood and primary schools can result in a decreased number of inappropriate behaviors, disciplinary consequences, and bullying incidents. Tiered behavioral supports require a consistent and fair approach to student discipline. Students who need a more targeted approach could take part in small group interventions. School counselors and social workers often host small groups that target student behaviors. As an example, these small groups may focus on making friends or understanding boundaries. When a student needs a more targeted and customized intervention, they may also meet on a one-on-one basis with the school counselor or the school social worker. Student behavior is linked to and impacts student achievement. As such, concerning behaviors must be addressed to ensure that learning opportunities can successfully occur. Instituting a system through which students learn how to self-regulate or monitor their own emotions and behaviors will result in a learning environment that is conducive to learning.

It is important for you to familiarize yourself with how your teachers, grade level teams, and staff members ensure that all students are receiving the support they need to be successful. As the building leader, you must also advocate for targeted, differentiated instruction for students. This is to be inclusive of struggling students, English language learners, students with special needs, students identified as academically gifted, and students in need of behavioral support.

Leadership tip: Invite your grade level teams to use the data obtained from progress monitoring to identify grade level trends and areas of strengths and weaknesses. This will enable your teams to collaborate, solve problems of practice, and design data-driven instruction. Frequently check in with your teams and be informed of what the data says about your building. Also, ask your team if they can identify your school's core values. If not, draft a list of core values that are expected of students and members of the school community. Common examples include, but are not limited to respect, honesty, caring, etc.

All Learning Is Social and Emotional

Before we begin to discuss how all learning is social and emotional, it is important to establish a sound definition of social and emotional learning. The Collaborative for Academic, Social, and Emotional Learning (CASEL) defines social and emotional learning as follows:

> Social and emotional learning (SEL) is the process through which all young people and adults acquire and apply the knowledge, skills, and attitudes to develop healthy identities, manage emotions and achieve personal and collective goals, feel, and show empathy for others, establish and maintain supportive relationships, and make responsible and caring decisions.
>
> (CASEL, 2021)

CASEL asserts that including social and emotional learning as an important component of schooling will yield improved academic outcomes and behaviors because the focus is on establishing learning environments where students feel safe, valued, and have a collective sense of belonging. In *All Learning Is Social and Emotional: Helping Students Develop Essential Skills for the Classroom and Beyond* (2019), Frey, Fisher, and Smith extend this framework to also consider unique perspectives around literacy. Becoming familiar with these models will allow you as a school leader to decide what aspects are important to your school community. If you recall in Chapter 1, we discussed Maslow's hierarchy of needs which suggested that students' basic needs must be met for them to be able to focus on learning and eventually achieve self-actualization. By infusing social and emotional learning opportunities in classrooms, educators can guide students toward achieving success.

CASEL has identified five areas of social and emotional competencies that help guide this practice. These include self-awareness, self-management, social awareness, relationship skills, and responsible decision making. Infusing SEL lessons as a component of classroom instruction calls for the explicit teaching of skills that could be used during learning, while playing, and at home or within the community. *We have included the CASEL website under Our Favorite Resources section for you to peruse and gather ideas to help you incorporate SEL within your school and across the curriculum.* The following are three daily opportunities that are conducive to embedding social and emotional learning into daily instruction:

Morning message time: The morning message is an important component in early childhood and primary classrooms as it sets the tone for the children's instructional day. Invite your teachers to share positive affirmations, lead students in the use of strategies to regulate their emotions, and teach them how to make responsible choices. The morning message is a brief classroom activity that typically precedes a read aloud or calendar time.

Read aloud time: Another constant in early childhood and primary classrooms are read alouds. Mentor texts are carefully curated for this time. Guide your classroom teachers to intentionally select mentor texts that elicit thinking, allow for opportunities to problem-solve in the social development areas like getting along, showing kindness, and practicing self-awareness. Utilize this time to reaffirm some of the positive behaviors you have seen throughout the school day.

Brain breaks: Brain breaks are another must in early childhood and primary school settings! Students need breaks throughout the day.

Classroom teachers could incorporate mindfulness activities into these sessions. Breathing techniques, meditation, and yoga are great activities for transition times. They allow students to get up, move around, and get mentally ready for the next activity. Brain breaks can be used to teach students how to regulate their emotions and behaviors.

Leadership tip: Set up a monthly principal's mentor text. The text could be a picture book, poem, or mantra that could be used to teach a skill, strategy, or to give a specific message to your students. Teachers can read the text to students at the beginning of the month and you as the leader can use this opportunity to generate discussions with your students, provide positive affirmations during morning announcements, or invite students to submit reading responses for you to highlight on your bulletin board. For example, using the read aloud *Mr. Posey's New Glasses* by Ted Kooser, a school leader can reinforce the affirmation: "I can see things in a whole new way." While this mentor text begins with a main character who struggles with depression, it is friends in the community who help him to see things in a new light.

Helpful resources: Check out www.readtothem.org for useful tips and strategies on how to get started with a One School, One Book initiative. While this initiative is not required for emphasizing SEL, it certainly helps to engage the school community around common texts with shareable and relatable messages.

Engaging around Inclusivity

In this chapter, we have discussed how multi-tiered supports provide students with the support they need to successfully learn and apply content. We also spoke about CASEL's framework and the notion that all learning is social and emotional. As we shift our discussion to focus on engaging students through inclusive practices, keep in mind that SEL also involves a commitment to equity and excellence. CASEL, for example, recognizes the work of scholars who are advocating for "transformative SEL, which challenges SEL within systems that are inequitable": https://casel.org/fundamentals-of-sel/how-does-sel-support-educational-equity-and-excellence/transformative-sel/.

Leadership tip: Prepare various models of SEL to share with your key stakeholders. Create a T-chart to draft the strengths and limitations of various models. Develop a plan to share your school's vision for ensuring that all students' social, emotional, and academic learning needs are met. Be sure to spotlight the cultural assets of the community in which you lead.

As you become more aware of the importance of SEL, you will likely find yourself in constant reflection around whose needs are met and how you are working toward ensuring that all students are and feel included in your school community. In the field of education, inclusive practice refers to the idea that all students, regardless of learning disabilities or language acquisition skills, can participate and engage in the same learning environment as their general education peers. The premise is that students in inclusive settings learn at a higher rate because they have the potential to learn with and from their peers. It is important for our students in inclusive settings to feel a sense of belonging. Proper planning, consideration, and preparation need to be provided to ensure that all students are making academic gains.

Below, we discuss three strategies that help drive the success of inclusive practices in school settings:

> **Guided reading and guided math**: During guided reading or guided math groups, a select group of students consisting of no more than five to six students is working alongside a teacher. These students are on the same reading or math levels. The teacher works to support students as they make gains toward reaching the grade level standards. When done consistently and correctly, guided instruction has the potential to elevate students' success. Keys to effective guided reading or mathematics instructions include actively monitoring student progress, providing the appropriate scaffolds, and consistent instruction.

> **Strategy groupings**: During strategy groupings, a select group of students consisting of no more than five to six students is working alongside a teacher. These students do not have to be on the same reading or math proficiency levels. Rather, the commonality with strategy groupings is that the students may need support with a specific skill or strategy. Strategy groupings allow for mixed ability groupings. This gives your teachers some flexibility in forming groups. When done intentionally, strategy groupings facilitate student interactions,

enable academic discourse, and build resiliency among young learners. Similar to guided reading and math, strategy groupings must incorporate active monitoring of student progress, appropriate scaffolds, and consistent instruction.

Universal Design for Learning (UDL): Educators who utilize UDL begin with the end in mind. They think about their students' strengths, weaknesses, language abilities, program needs, and prior learning experiences. They then incorporate scaffolds and appropriate supports to ensure that all students have the potential to comprehend and be successful with the lessons being taught.

Leadership tip: Promote the use of a lesson plan template that allows teachers to incorporate opportunities for guided reading/math, strategy groupings, and different instructional strategies that will help students succeed. If a template like this is not already utilized in your school, reach out to your literacy and math colleagues for suggestions. Many leaders stay connected to other leaders in their regions/states. Determine if an email list is in use in your area for troubleshooting questions and looking for important resources.

Eye on equity: Students' social, emotional, and academic growth requires a great deal of planning. As an instructional leader, it is imperative that you review your school's curriculum, curricular resources, and instructional practices. Careful consideration must be given to how your school addresses students' needs. You may want to consider the following: What strategies are in place to help students who struggle? How are those strategies used in the classroom? How does your early childhood setting handle student discipline? How are you fostering a sense of community and belonging in your respective school setting?

The Role of Play in Learning

Thus far, this chapter focused on discussing how multi-tiered supports can be implemented to guide the social, emotional, and academic development of our early learners. We identified morning message time, read aloud time, and brain breaks as opportunities to infuse social and emotional learning into instruction. We also identified guided reading, guided math, strategy groupings, and the use of UDL as instructional practices that facilitate inclusivity. We now highlight the role of play in enhancing learning, socialization, emotional growth, and development in children. Recall that children undergo changes in the cognitive, physical, communication, speech, social, and emotional domains as they grow through the different stages of development.

According to the National Association for the Education of Young Children (2021), "play and learning go hand in hand … they are intertwined … they are like a science lecture with a lab … play is the lab." This description of the role of play in learning is short, yet powerful. Providing children with opportunities to play can result in classroom and school-wide learning gains with a bonus side effect of joy. Understanding the role of play in learning and development will help you create learning institutions that allow educators to use play as a means of enhancing child development. When children engage in play, they activate their imagination and begin to think creatively. Play is an opportunity to bridge joy with learning. Other positive side effects of play include the ability to problem-solve, improved socialization skills, critical thinking skills, and the ability to focus while persevering on a task (Gronlund, 2021).

Incorporating Play in Classrooms

In our experiences teaching and leading in early childhood settings, we have come across several ways in which teachers have successfully incorporated play as a part of the instructional day. While the following two suggestions are not exhaustive, we hope they will serve as a starting point for you to begin to think creatively and to generate ideas on how your school can enhance children's learning experiences through play.

> **Centers:** We briefly touched upon learning centers as means to provide students with opportunities to practice skills learned in class. However, centers can also be utilized to provide children with opportunities to engage in play. In early childhood, we have seen dramatic play come to life through storytelling centers adorned with puppets, props, and different trinkets that helped activate children's imagination and creativity while playing. We have also seen teachers transform academic skills into games that students enjoy playing either independently or with peers. Skills such as phonemic awareness, letter identification, rhyming, blending, and sound segmentation can be practiced through board games and puzzles. Center time is the perfect time to allow children to practice learning through play. Careful planning and intentionality

must take place to effectively execute play centers that are meaningful and engaging for students.

Suggestions for centers:

- Dramatic play
- Puzzles
- Games
- Manipulatives
- Sorts (word sorts/sound sorts/shape sorts)
- Drawing/painting

Play breaks: We know that children need breaks and opportunities to move around. Incorporating movement throughout the day can help generate increased motivation, engagement, and learning. If you are in an area with warm weather, bringing children outside for ten minutes of playtime can increase children's happiness levels and promote their social development. In months when you cannot get the children outside, the gymnasium or play-based rooms could serve as alternative locations to help facilitate play breaks and increase happiness in students. However, opportunities for play can occur in your regular classrooms as well. The key is in allowing students to engage in play for a few minutes of the day. Infusing play breaks into the school day provides children with something special to look forward to.

Suggestions for play breaks:

- Dancing (GoNoodle is excellent and can be accessed via www.gonoodle .com)
- Running (could be running in place just to get the jitters out)
- Play dough
- Sand table
- Water table
- Manipulatives
- Blocks

Leadership tip: Play breaks could also serve as opportunities for early childhood leaders to engage with and learn more about the students they serve. Keep your grade level teams' schedules readily available. Try to join in and see what students are doing, talking about, and dreaming of during their play breaks. Your presence will help you build positive relationships with your students. Those relationships will result in the creation of a positive school culture that values children's social, emotional, and academic development.

Eye on equity: It is important to continuously promote and work on cultivating a sense of belongingness in classrooms and schools. Therefore, look to find inclusive resources for your centers and play areas. You may want to consider games that are conducive to children's needs, that are representative of their cultures, and that promote a sense of inclusion. For example, consider adding multicultural tools, play accessories, and toys. One of our favorite tools are multicultural crayons made by Crayola.

Final Thoughts

This chapter focused on affirming the notion that students undergo changes and that those changes can be identified through an understanding of developmental milestones. We provided an outline identifying developmental milestones that are driven by the cognitive, physical, communication, speech, social, and emotional domains. We suggested the use of multi-tier supports when children demonstrate a lag in reaching a respective milestone. A multi-tier support strategy should be implemented when students need intervention in either academics or behaviors. The need for interventions must be student centered and geared toward helping students make progress on ascertaining the skills characterized by their developmental stage and respective milestone.

We continued by posing the idea that all learning is social and emotional. Therefore, we call for the integration of opportunities for social and emotional learning into daily instruction. The morning message, read-aloud time, and brain breaks are perfect opportunities to explicitly and intentionally work on social and emotional development strategies with students.

Considering the diversity of students within any given early childhood and primary classroom or school, it is important to utilize instructional strategies that are inclusive. Guided reading, guided math, strategy groupings, and Universal Design for Learning are strategies that allow for student-centered instruction as well as intentional and targeted differentiation. Finally, integrating play into the school day through centers and intentional opportunities for students to play allows them to develop a joy for learning and can promote a sense of belonging and positive school culture.

- Collaborative for Academic, Social, and Emotional Learning (CASEL) https://casel.org
- Positiveaction.net
- Readtothem.org

Chapter 3: Reflection Questions

- What systems are in place to help my teachers and grade level teams meet the needs of students?
- Are there strategies in place to support the social and emotional development of all?
- How are my grade level teams addressing behavior concerns?
- How am I promoting an inclusive learning environment?

Chapter 3: Promoting Students' Social, Emotional, and Academic Growth Leadership Action Spotlight

Identify three takeaways from Chapter 3.

_____

_____

_____

Write down two ideas that you would like to implement in your current role.

OR for aspiring leaders

Write down two ideas that you would consider implementing in the future.

_____
_____
_____

Identify one lingering question or area you would like to explore further.

_____
_____
_____

Personal reflection, thoughts, comments, concerns, ideas:

_____
_____
_____
_____
_____

Understanding Teaching, Learning, Student Engagement, and Recognition in Early Childhood Settings

Standing Out as a "Lit" Early Childhood Leader

Positive Affirmation: I Can Ignite a Love for Learning

Love is a feeling that propels you to respond, to experience, and to achieve. It is a powerful force that kindles the soul's purpose. Leading with love requires you to acknowledge, accept, and affirm students as they are. Lead with love and you will help establish a solid foundation for growth, development, and success. Love is contagious, and your actions are bound to ignite your students' love for learning.

****

Literacy Learning in Early Childhood Spaces

Literacy encompasses the ability to read, write, speak, and listen. As such, literacy is the foundation of all learning. To improve student outcomes, effective literacy practices must be in place in early childhood spaces. Early childhood leaders must take part in creating learning environments that are literacy centered. While this is not an extensive list, we will briefly introduce the five literacy practices that should be embedded in the early childhood and primary school day. These practices set the foundation for students to learn to read so that they can successfully make the transition to reading to learn in the intermediate elementary grades.

DOI: 10.4324/9781003219767-6

Reading: Reading sets the foundation for learning. Students in early childhood can be engaged in opportunities where they listen to reading or participate in the sharing of reading. Through shared reading opportunities, children learn to practice skills and strategies that will support their ability to read independently. Learning the alphabet, phonemic awareness, and word recognition are skills enhanced by and developed through reading. Children must have access to high-interest books as well as decodable texts to practice with. Embedding opportunities for students to have a choice in text selection enhances their motivation to practice and engage in reading.

Writing: Children should be able to make the connection between reading and writing. They should view writing as a means of expressing their ideas on paper. During the early stages of writing, children should be encouraged to use pictures and labels to depict their thoughts. As they grow and develop their early writing abilities, sentences can begin to be included. Allow opportunities for students to write their own stories. Provide them with developmentally appropriate writing paper and tools to facilitate the process. Support their attempts by providing them with positive affirmations and validating their work.

Speaking/listening: Speaking and listening are crucial to language development. Children should have plenty of opportunities to listen to stories, share their insights, and practice oral language development by using the language and vocabulary they hear in stories. Create a dramatic play center. Provide students with props and accessories that will help activate their creativity and imagination. Allow them to share their oral stories with peers. Validate their imagination and support their attempts at both listening to others and expressing their own oral stories.

Viewing: Students should be able to make sense of multimedia, including, but not limited to videos, images (e.g. illustrations, photographs), news, environments, and visuals in the environment. Environmental print is seen by students on a daily basis. In fact, many toddlers learn to identify and essentially read signs like "McDonalds" way before they learn the alphabet. Leverage the use of multimedia and environmental print to connect letter recognition to sounds and eventually to reading.

Leadership tip: To develop the literacy skills and areas noted in this chapter, consider the use of literacy centers to allow students to (1) socialize and co-construct knowledge with others, (2) reinforce skills and strategies learned in the classroom, and (3) develop skills around engaging in academic ways. When children engage in play, they activate their imagination. It is during this special time that children leverage their experiences and express themselves freely. They use content-specific vocabulary, descriptions, and role play and collaborate with peers. This time can be semi-structured so that children are not just playing for the sake of playing. The activities that they are engaged in call for the practice or review of targeted and specific skills. Refer back to Chapter 4 to review our discussion on the role of play in early childhood.

    Leadership tip: In *Breaking through the Language Arts Block: Organizing and Managing the Exemplary Literacy Day* (2018), Morrow, Kunz, and Hall introduced different structures for promoting literacy in early childhood and elementary environments. Many professional texts can support your and your team's professional development. Consider a book club format for digging deeper in this area.

Literacy Best Practices in Early Childhood Classrooms
Consider researching to learn more about the following components for
   integrating comprehensive literacy in early childhood classrooms:
Phonological/phonemic awareness
Phonics
Fluency
Vocabulary
Comprehension
Writing
Motivation, engagement, and joy

Literacy must be at the forefront of early childhood and primary school learning. Children who learn to read will be prepared to make the transition of reading to learn, grow, and develop. Now that you are aware of the literacy practices that must be utilized in daily early childhood classroom instruction, let's shift the focus to how you can promote a literacy-centered early childhood school setting.

Becoming a "Lit" Literacy Leader

A "lit" leader is someone that embodies excellence in and promotes a love for literacy practices that help students develop their literacy skills. "Lit" leaders motivate their students and staff to engage in and generate a love for literacy. The following strategies will help you become a "lit" leader among your students, teachers, and staff.

> **Literacy instruction**: As the instructional leader, you must be in tune with what is occurring in your classrooms. Literacy instruction should be taking place during a designated block of time and have extended opportunities for practice and reinforcement throughout the day. Explicit teaching of reading skills, strategies, vocabulary, and language development should be incorporated into the core of the literacy schedule. You should observe your teachers engaged in literacy instruction that is developmentally appropriate to the age groups they teach.
>
> Additionally, teachers should also be observed providing differentiated tailored instruction to students who need additional support. Evidence of scaffolding and vocabulary development should be visible throughout the classroom. Anchor charts, word walls/ sound walls, and clearly labeled and organized play areas are conducive to rich print environments essential to literacy development. Differentiated literacy instruction must be responsive to students' needs, provided upon identifying gaps in learning, and inclusive of learners who need remediation or acceleration of skills and strategies.

Leadership tip: Consider creating a checklist for observing the quality of literacy instruction in your school community. Based on the Classroom Literacy Observation Schedule (CLOS) by Louden and Rohl (2008), you can take anecdotal notes based on different observable literacy dimensions.

1. Respect: Does the community of readers/writers function in a warm, welcoming, and respectful environment? Is intention communicated to the students in order to create a "flow"? Are equity and respect for diversity emphasized?

2. Knowledge: Does the lesson address key learning standards? Is a clear and student-friendly purpose and lesson explanation provided? Are strategies and concepts taught in an appropriate amount of time and with appropriate "chunking"? Are opportunities for developing oral language through talking provided? Are opportunities for developing written language provided?

3. Orchestration: Are students actively engaged and participating in the literacy block? How is the physical environment utilized and structured? Are key components of a comprehensive literacy program included? What opportunities exist for independent, small group, and partner practice?

4. Support: How is learning measured? Is a gradual release of responsibility model utilized? How is learning reinforced and practiced? What about students who need additional support?

5. Differentiation: Are choice, challenge, and individual needs taken into consideration? How are high, average, and low performing groups of students supported? Do questions posed to the learners represent different levels when it comes to depth of knowledge?

   Access to literacy: A well-stocked, neat, inviting, and culturally responsive classroom library should also be present in a literacy driven classroom. The classroom library should contain a range of books encompassing different reading levels, genres, and topics. Picture books, decodable books, age-appropriate informational texts, and early chapter books are among children's favorite texts to explore. Students should be provided with opportunities to select and engage with books of their own choosing. Giving them a choice in the types of books they read can help increase their intrinsic motivation to learn to read and persevere as they encounter new words. Pop into your literacy classrooms and check in with students. Ask questions about what they are reading, who their favorite characters are, and what they think they will read next. Make them feel that you genuinely value reading and love to hear them share their perspectives.

Some of Our Favorite Resources for Culturally Relevant Text Collections
We Need Diverse Books
https://diversebooks.org/
Little Free Library Read in Color Initiative
https://littlefreelibrary.org/read-in-color/
All Learning Is Social and Emotional: Helping Students Develop Essential Skills for the Classroom and Beyond (2019) by Frey, Fisher, and Smith (Extensive Appendix Included)
GoodReads
https://www.goodreads.com/list/tag/diversity
American Library Association
https://www.ala.org/advocacy/literacy/inclusive-booklists
Edutopia
https://www.edutopia.org/article/22-diverse-book-choices-all-grade-levels
Lee & Low Books
https://www.leeandlow.com/educators/reading-lists
Diverse BookFinder
https://diversebookfinder.org/

Teacher professional development: Investing in your teachers is investing in your students. To ensure that students are taught using effective instructional strategies, you must seek to understand your teachers' level of comfort in teaching students how to read. Professional development is an integral component for the effective teaching of reading. Teachers need to be effectively trained on the use of reading and writing strategies, using formative assessments to drive their differentiated small groups, and in developing learning environments that motivate students to apply the strategies learned. Professional development should be an ongoing process. Teachers must be provided with opportunities to participate in grade level meetings, share out problems of practice, and engage in collaborative discussions to help enhance student learning. Depending on the type of professional development, you may find yourself leading or facilitating the discussion.

Family engagement: Incorporating families into the school community is important as families play an integral role in supporting literacy practices. Keep family informed through electronic newsletters. Let them know the monthly literacy themes, key skills, and strategies, and suggest genres for them to explore alongside their children. Ensure that your newsletters are made available in the native languages spoken at home. Parents who are made aware of topics, themes, skills, and strategies could enlist the help of the public library to facilitate the selection of age-appropriate books for children. Another way to ensure that families are actively engaged with and connected to school happenings is through family literacy nights. During these special events your teacher teams can facilitate parent workshop sessions on specific reading strategies while the children enjoy a read aloud conducted by you, their "lit" instructional leader.

Through a grasp on effective literacy instruction, you will facilitate work that is driven by the needs of the students. You will ensure that students have access to literacy materials that pique their interests and allow them to practice reading skills. You will understand your teachers' needs and facilitate appropriate professional development to enhance their teaching capacity. By engaging families in literacy events, you will create a positive home and school connection that will improve students' literacy development.

Final Thoughts

A major focus of early childhood and primary school is developing and enhancing students' reading abilities to prepare them to make the shift from learning to read toward reading to learn in the intermediate grades. Key strategies deployed in literacy instruction include opportunities for speaking/listening, reading, writing, and play/center time. We concluded the chapter by providing suggestions on how you can become a "lit" leader and be in tune with best literacy teaching practices, strategies for providing students access to literacy, effective professional development for their teachers and staff, and opportunities for parents to be engaged in literacy learning.

Chapter 4: Reflection Questions

- Are my teachers' literacy schedules conducive to the needs of the students?

- Are teachers conducting small group instruction? If so, how often?
- Are the classrooms print rich and inclusive of students' developmental needs?
- How am I promoting literacy practices in school?
- How am I engaging families and advocating for an ongoing partnership?

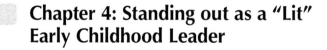

Chapter 4: Standing out as a "Lit" Early Childhood Leader

Leadership Action Spotlight

Identify three takeaways from Chapter 4.

_____

_____

_____

Write down two ideas that you would like to implement in your current role.

OR for aspiring leaders

Write down two ideas that you would consider implementing in the future.

_____

_____

_____

Identify one lingering question or area you would like to explore further.

_____

_____

_____

Personal reflection, thoughts, comments, concerns, ideas:

_____

_____

_____

_____

_____

Learning and Leading Strategies to Support Content Area Instruction

Positive Affirmation: I Can Design a Learning Agenda
That Builds Students' Background Knowledge and Passion
for Critical Thinking

Curriculum should help children make a deeper and fuller
understanding of their own experience—Lilian Katz.

Understanding a Need for Work in the Content Areas

As we consider lessons learned in early childhood related to literacy, it is crucial to understand that students in general need more access to (1) high-quality informational texts, (2) project-based instruction (PBI), and (3) thematic connections across the curriculum. Leaders in early childhood environments should understand that:

- Children deserve access to a balance of information and fiction in both print and digital formats.

- Thematic instruction and project-based instruction differ in that themes (e.g. weather, animals, friendship) can last for a shorter time whereas PBI can help to solve local problems through student-driven research and action over a longer period of time. In this chapter, we focus on the long-term learning associated with protecting the environment and thinking about the role of "Becoming an Aquanaut."

- Specific standards drive learning in the early childhood content areas.

DOI: 10.4324/9781003219767-7

- Standards also often encompass a set of skills that are 21st century based and necessary for success in future college and career pathways. These standards also include the use of technology.

Literacy/Language Arts "Beyond the Block"

In Chapter 4, you were introduced to the importance of being a "lit" leader, equipped to prioritize the reading, writing, speaking, listening, and viewing skills of emergent/early readers and writers. In addition to the bulleted tips above, consider the following opportunities to connect literacy to content area instruction.

Mentor Text Title and Author	Reading Strategy	Writing Strategy	Content Area Learning Standards	Content Area Skills	Digital Resource

Using this template, early childhood leaders can help teachers reflect on the following:

- What subject matter or content area is the focus for instruction?
- Do certain mentor texts further highlight information about our current topic of study?
- What reading and/or writing strategies connect to this study and connect students to their existing goals as readers or writers?
- What content area learning standards are important for this grade level and area of study?
- What else should students be able to do in this content area?
- Do digital resources support teaching and understanding in this area?

Below is an example of this type of planning in action. The outline combines literacy, science, and math, as students become "aquanauts" concerned about the environment and protecting our oceans. This lesson was developed in partnership with the Fabien Cousteau Ocean Learning Center (FCOLC) and represents a developmentally appropriate focus for students in grades K–2.

Unpacking a Lesson: Who Is the Mystery Person?

In this lesson, students begin by looking closely at a photograph of an aquanaut. Students can independently think about who the person is and what they might be doing. The teacher can collect students' ideas and jot them down on post-it notes to support students who are not quite able to write on their own. Students who are able can write and label their ideas on a post-it note independently. Ideas can be posted on a chart under the column "What I Think I Know …"

Students are reminded that in today's lesson the identity, or who the person in the photograph is, will be revealed based on clues that they notice in the video.

Look at the photograph and think about who this person is and what they might be doing.					
What I Think I Know …	Confirmed Learning +	Misconceptions –	I Still Wonder …	New Learning	How to Find out … READ RESEARCH REACH OUT TO AN EXPERT

After watching a video about underwater exploration by aquanauts, the teacher can facilitate a conversation with the students. Do their post-it notes move to "confirmed learning" or are there some misconceptions? Choose a few of the post-it notes to discuss in depth. Summarize some of the findings with the students. Next, distribute post-it notes to have the students jot down something new they have learned or a question they still have.

 # Introduce the Discovery Affirmation

What Is a Discovery Affirmation?

An affirmation gives students words of encouragement as they affirm, or assert strong beliefs about something important to them. In this lesson, students affirm and discover that (1) they can identify as scientists and (2) be problem solvers. Affirmations can be used across content areas and encourage students to say "yes" to themselves as scholars.

As a scientist, I believe there are no impossible missions, only possible solutions.

In this lesson design, it is important to note that the focus on the content area and learning standards is first and foremost. Students are expected to be able to model Earth and human activity and develop deeper connections about plants, animals, and human interactions. Using the reading and analyzing nonfiction (RAN) strategy, students are drawn into the lesson to reflect on their initial understandings about aquanauts. Later, a mentor text and digital resources are used to further wonder and inquire about the topic. A daily affirmation for social and emotional learning (SEL) is included so that students personally identify as scientists. In addition, literacy skills related to reading and writing are integrated in the lesson.

Leadership tip: When you first take on the role of educational leader, it can be overwhelming to become acclimated to your workplace and district policies. At the same time, it is important to understand what curricular programs impact your students. Create binders or digital folders to organize the existing content area maps in content areas that fall under your purview. These resource collections can be referenced when it comes to the future design of professional learning opportunities or ensuring compliance with local, state, and federal mandates affecting teaching and learning in the content areas.

Focusing on Mathematics

Effective mathematics instruction in early childhood and primary schools is critical to instill a solid math foundation within students. Early childhood educators should approach teaching math concepts with positivity and joy. As young learners begin to explore and develop math concepts, they achieve a sense of how mathematics is utilized in everyday life. While not all early childhood and primary schools operate the same or utilize the same resources, we have generated brief descriptions of what we have observed in an effective early childhood mathematics classroom. While the following list of strategies is not exhaustive, it will facilitate your thinking and reflecting on how your respective early childhood setting incorporates the teaching of mathematics into classroom instruction.

Consider the lesson presented earlier in this chapter. To further develop the lesson and students' exposure to mathematical concepts, school leaders

Table 5.1 Suggested Resources for Unpacking the Early Childhood Learning Environment

Mentor Text Title and Author	Reading Strategy	Writing Strategy	Content Area Learning Standards	Content Area Skills	Digital Resource
Astronaut-Aquanaut: How Space Science and Sea Science Interact by Jennifer Swanson	Reading and analyzing nonfiction	Quickwrite	K-ESS3-1 Earth and Human Activity: Use a model to represent the relationship between the needs of different plants and animals (including humans) and the places they live	Modeling	Fabien Cousteau Ocean Learning Center (FCOLC) https://www .fabiencousteauolc.org/ about-us

should consider the following six tips for enhancing students' mathematical understanding:

Six Strategies for Enhancing Students' Mathematical Understanding

1. Differentiate learning by exploring prior, current, and future grade-level expectations.
2. Assess student learning to identify areas of needed support. Reinforce these key areas across time to ensure that understanding is committed to students' long-term, and not short-term memory.
3. Incorporate ways for students to develop fluency in math.
4. Scaffold with appropriate strategies (including teacher-created guides).
5. Create authentic problems for students to solve.
6. Celebrate a focus on mathematical vocabulary.

Leadership tip: Organizations such as the National Council of Teachers of Mathematics provide position statements about the teaching of math (https://www.nctm.org/). By becoming a part of their network, you will begin to consider ways of enhancing math instruction in your learning community. For example, one position statement advocates for having a math specialist at the elementary level. Consider how having this type of role in your building might help students reach their goals.

Understanding Regulations

As you continue to explore best practices related to early childhood content instruction, you must also recognize that many local and state requirements impact a variety of areas related to content area instruction. These can include (1) curriculum laws, (2) regulations related to time allocated to certain requirements (e.g. recess), (3) health and safety laws, (4) laws regarding special education, (5) professional development requirements, (6) textbook adoptions, and (7) testing considerations. It is important for early childhood leaders to become familiar with the specific policies and regulations impacting one's role in a school. Because these regulations change and are updated annually, the authors recommend being an active member of a local association with programs aimed at further developing school leaders' understanding of these regulations and how they impact early childhood education.

 ## Making Curricular Choices

Educational leaders are also often assigned the awesome responsibility of getting to choose programs and resources to enhance the educational program. In Chapter 8, we introduce the What Works Clearinghouse as one potential resource for vetting quality materials. We also believe in the power and promise of gathering stakeholders from your school community to pilot resources, and even organically build programs that are best suited for your young learners. In one of our proud partner schools, this took on a life of its own as a new kindergarten program was exploring options for integrating social studies within the school day. Under the leadership of their supervisor Gina Schiano, the kindergarten team refined lessons throughout the year according to the units/topics calendar below.

These units were unpacked with the following features to enhance learning across the curriculum:

- Interactive read alouds
- Opportunities for students to respond to reading
- Shared reading with vocabulary enriched messages
- Shared writing
- Poetry
- Project-based learning (PBL) opportunities

 ## Sample Kindergarten Integrated Social Studies Themes/Units

Unit 1: We Are Kindergarten Citizens
Unit 2: Gracias, We Are Thankful
Unit 3: Families, Traditions, and Holidays
Unit 4: Needs and Wants
Unit 5: Maps and Globes
Unit 6: Juneteenth Jamboree

By reflecting on the implementation of the organically grown units across the year, teachers were able to take pride in creating student work displays while also considering ways to adapt and revise the lessons for future learners. Best of all, the team was able to create a curriculum that addressed the state standards for the content area while also integrating a focus on literacy and culturally responsive instruction.

Eye on equity: As we reflect on our curricular programming, it is important for early childhood leaders to understand that from a gender equity perspective, representation of women is not always equitable across the curriculum. When you consider the lesson presented earlier in this chapter, it is important to understand that many young women do not associate themselves with becoming scientists or mathematicians. As a matter of fact, the STEM fields are still heavily male dominated, as women make up approximately 28% of the workforce (https://www.aauw.org/resources/research/the-stem-gap/). Gender stereotypes, fewer role models, and anxiety around math are key to the problem. To address this, we need to consider how early childhood environments can change that narrative. In the lesson introduced in this chapter, *all* students are invited to see themselves as scientists, or, in this case, aquanauts. Materials shared by the FCOLC also include videos that highlight a gender-diverse field of aquanauts. In February, perhaps your school community could celebrate International Day of Women and Girls in Science on February 11 (https://www.un.org/en/observances/women-and-girls-in-science-day). The digital world has made it possible to virtually connect with female role models from around the world. The possibilities are endless, and equitable learning opportunities exist if explored and implemented.

Leadership tip: In this chapter, we introduce a sample kindergarten scope and sequence for integrated social studies throughout the year. Take a look at the unit titles and consider ways in which gender equity can be addressed across the topics. For example, when looking at the unit on "We Are Kindergarten Citizens," can you think of any local women leaders who are citizens in your community that students could be introduced to? What diverse books can enhance student learning across this unit?

Final Thoughts

In this chapter, we advocate for literacy experiences that extend beyond the traditional reading block. We know that learners flourish when opportunities to read, write, speak, listen, and view are intentionally designed across the school day and throughout other areas of instruction. We introduce a STEM-based lesson where students have an opportunity to engage, wonder, and think critically about a standards-based topic. At the same time, we implore school leaders to design a culture around joy in math while breaking down any barriers preventing all students from succeeding. In the reflection section that follows, we encourage you to think about other content areas you want to learn more about. Understand that early childhood development encompasses many key areas including, but not limited to, creative arts, physical education, health education, and problem solving in general. As you connect with the adults working in your school building, take pride in knowing that each of these individuals plays a crucial role in helping the whole child develop. Embrace their funds of knowledge, fuel their passion for lifelong learning, and celebrate alongside teachers and students as they share their ideas and new learning.

Chapter 5: Reflection Questions

- When you look back on your preparation as a teacher or educational leader, what subject areas are a strength in your toolkit? What areas would you like to learn more about?

- What opportunities exist in your school year for curriculum development teams to meet and explore issues raised in this chapter, among others that are presented in your individual school community?

- Are there any gaps that exist in your educational programming?

- How else might you ensure that your budding scholars are receiving a strong foundation for future college and career success?

- Is an emphasis on social and emotional learning (SEL) evident throughout curricular programs?

- What other content is needed for your young learners?

Chapter 5: Learning and Leading Strategies to Support Content Area Instruction

Leadership Action Spotlight

Identify three takeaways from Chapter 5.

_____

_____

_____

Write down two ideas that you would like to implement in your current role.

OR for aspiring leaders

Write down two ideas that you would consider implementing in the future.

_____

_____

_____

Identify one lingering question or area you would like to explore further.

_____

_____

_____

Personal reflection, thoughts, comments, concerns, ideas:

_____

_____

_____

_____

Spotting and Recognizing Student Engagement and Intentional Learning

Positive Affirmation: I Feel Accomplished When Students Are Learning

The goal of school leaders is to ensure students are learning. Considering the differences in stages of development coupled with the varied learning styles, learning looks different in every classroom. As an early childhood leader, you will have an opportunity to see academic, social, and emotional growth in action. Your experiences as the instructional leader should consist of joy, pride, and a sense of accomplishment. Do not disregard these feelings. Your students are learning because YOU are creating an environment that is conducive to their needs. That is an excellent reason to feel accomplished.

****

Engaging the "Whole Child"

As cliché as it sounds, it is important to acknowledge and engage the "whole child." Before we get any further, let's unpack what is meant by the term "whole child." Engaging the whole child references the notion that children have various needs, come from diverse home environments, and require a myriad of strategies to ensure they are provided with opportunities to learn and grow both socially and academically. No two children are alike, thus, learning can look differently from child to child. When thinking about educating the whole child, we want you to consider the following questions:

- Are your students being challenged?
- Do students feel seen, included, and a part of your school?
- Are their stories reflected in the curriculum?

DOI: 10.4324/9781003219767-8

- Do they feel like your school is a safe zone?
- Does your school facilitate opportunities for students to engage with peers?
- How are families included and a part of the learning zone?
- What role does the community play in the overall operation of your school?

When you think about these questions and take the time to reflect on your responses, you begin to understand that school is not just about academics. Think of your school building as a magical place that can serve to elevate children's wildest dreams. As the leader, it is up to you to help cultivate the magic that exists in early childhood and primary school settings. You set the tone for learning, engagement, and inclusivity.

Engaging the whole child requires leadership that is cognizant of the outside forces that play a role in and impact children's development. Consider taking an active role in understanding your school community. Research your community demographics, locate your school's community partners, and begin to build relationships that will allow for meaningful ways to recognize and engage students. Relationships with outside partners are not the only relationships you must be intentional about. Building relationships with parents, caregivers, and students alike will also help you understand and effectively advocate for academic instruction and school programming that meets the diverse needs of the students attending your school. When you establish a collaborative school environment, your students will know that you support them and are paving the way to an environment that guides them toward making positive choices while engaging in productive struggles through various learning experiences.

Leadership tip: Be visible outside of school, too. Your participation in community events such as parades or town gatherings will help you understand your students, the community, and their overall needs. Your visibility will reinforce your care and concern for students and help establish positive relationships. As you engage in the local community, lean into the assets of the community. In *Ethical Leadership in Schools: Creating Community in an Environment of Accountability*, Strike (2007) emphasizes that trust is a condition of community. As a leader, position yourself to engage in these events cooperatively and not competitively. Our integrity matters when we are visible in our communities.

Planning for Intentional Learning

Benjamin Franklin once said, "if you fail to plan, you are planning to fail." This sentiment holds true for early childhood and primary schools. There are many factors that need to be considered for students to be successful in their classrooms. As the leader, you are to be engaged and familiar with all aspects of learning in your building. Remember that because we are focused on the whole child, when we refer to learning we are not solely focused on academics. We also reference students' social and emotional learning as well. As a result, consider the following when planning for intentional learning opportunities:

Current Outside Issues Impacting Students

The world is constantly changing, and these changes can influence students' lives and impact their school performance. Consider for example the COVID-19 pandemic. One side effect of the pandemic was the devastating closure of brick-and-mortar schools giving way to virtual learning. For some, this did not cause much of a problem. For others, the pandemic created chaos and isolation, and shed light on the substantial inequities that impact our students. As a school leader, you must be aware of the happenings around your community. Collaborating with outside agencies and community partners can help you identify the situations occurring within the community that have an impact on students. When considering outside issues that impact students, ask yourself the following:

- Is there something happening outside of my school that is impacting my students? What is it?
- How can I help create an environment that supports students who are struggling?
- How can I help create an environment where students feel safe?
- How can I foster a positive home-to-school relationship between my school, parents, and caretakers?
- Am I creating opportunities for parents to share and express concerns that may be affecting students?

Giving parents an opportunity to share concerns, ask questions, and have input on possible solutions could provide you with valuable information as you seek to understand how outside forces impact students in your care. These actions give parents a voice, allow them to play an active role in solidifying the home-to-school relationship, and empower them to take action and be involved in their children's education.

School Curriculum and Curricular Resources

The school curriculum along with its corresponding curricular resources are tools used by classroom teachers to teach students the standards deemed essential to learning. To ascertain that your students are learning, you must familiarize yourself with all the components of your school's curriculum. These include but are not limited to learning intentions, success criteria, instructional activities, and pacing guides, as well as formative and summative assessments. You must carefully analyze how the curricular resources are conducive to the needs of the students you serve. In doing so, you may want to consider the following questions: *Are your students and their experiences reflected in the texts they listen to and read? Are the suggested activities conducive to the developmental needs of your learners? Are there opportunities for students to collaborate and ask questions? Do the assessments help guide your teacher's instructional decisions?*

From a curriculum perspective, it is also helpful to reflect on the following questions:

- Do teachers at each grade level have familiarity and comfort with their grade-level standards?
- Are standards translated to daily (concrete and measurable) learning objectives?
- Are student-friendly learning objectives and agendas posted daily in the classroom environment?
- Do teachers engage in short- and long-term planning around each curriculum area's scope and sequence?
- Are lesson templates used to plan? Ensure that lesson plans include opportunities for whole group, small group, and independent/partner work, and 1:1 opportunities for the teacher to confer with learners.
- Do classroom lessons include intentional opportunities for students to turn and talk about their learning?

There is a plethora of tools available to help early childhood leaders better understand teaching and learning in the early grades. These questions provide a great place to get started and to consider the needs of your school community. In Chapter 2, we emphasized that you are, indeed, not alone. If the needs assessed in these areas lead to numerous future areas for potential growth in your school community, reach out to trusted colleagues and consultants for support. Partnerships can truly enhance your school's curriculum and have positive learning outcomes for your young learners.

Teacher Needs and Development

Your teachers are an integral component of your school. Just like your students, your teachers will be in different stages of teaching and learning. At any given point, you may find yourself leading new teachers, veteran teachers, highly effective teachers, and ineffective ones too. In planning for intentional adult learning opportunities, you truly need to know your teaching staff. You need to assess, reflect upon, and elaborate about perceived areas of strength and weakness. To identify and speak to teacher needs, you must continue to enhance your own teaching repertoire to keep abreast of best teaching practices and innovative ideas that can assist in increasing student achievement.

Your preparation will also result in better conversations with your teacher teams. These conversations will be based on timely, actionable feedback that will result in the enhancement of their teaching practice. Your instructional leadership should pave the way for you to guide and support your teaching teams. Let them know and understand that your strength lies in a collective effort to engage in learning experiences that help move students toward success. Promote trying new strategies and implementing new ideas. Guide your teams through the process of self-reflection. In fact, reflection should be a frequently practiced component of teacher effectiveness. Model how to be reflective and identify the importance of reflection for overall school improvement.

Leadership tip: When introducing new initiatives or reviewing best practices in your school community, allow for the existence and creation of multiple goals. Consider the two curriculum and instruction goals in Table 6.1. While goal #1 may be more appropriate for a novice teacher, it could also be the focus of a teacher who is new to a grade level. Goal #2, on the other hand, is differentiated to raise levels of thinking around this sample initiative.

When selecting goals alongside teachers, remember to always (1) name teachers' strengths, (2) build on teachers' strengths, and (3) reiterate that when it comes to best practices, our goal is to be better each and every day when we show up for our young learners.

School Climate and Culture

School leaders are responsible for setting the tone of the school's climate and culture. A positive school climate and culture is critical for both students and

Table 6.1 Sample Curriculum Goal Chart with Multiple Goals That Teachers Can Use to Self-Identify for Professional Learning

---

Curriculum Goal 2023–2024

Diversity, Equity, and Inclusion in the Curriculum

Goal 1. I am able to use educational resources from trusted professional organizations to select reading materials suitable for grade-level learners when it comes to our state's emphasis on diversity, equity, and inclusion in the PreK–3 curriculum.

Goal 2. I am able to integrate multiple opportunities for fostering students' social and emotional learning (SEL) when planning lessons that affirm diversity, equity, and inclusion.

---

teachers as it paves the way for learning to occur. Think about the overall ambiance of your building. How do you want your students, teachers, and staff members to feel when they walk into your building? Do you want them to love coming to your school? Do you want them to feel like your school is a fair and equitable place to be? Are the rules and procedures put in place to benefit the whole and not just a few? Are you consistent in delivering positive affirmations and mantras? Do you engage your students, teachers, and staff in reviewing your schools' mission and vision? Do you set achievable goals? Do you praise? Do your actions demonstrate empathy, care, and concern for the well-being of others? These questions are important and must be considered when thinking about the culture of a school. To help guide this work, you can establish a School Improvement (ScIP) team. ScIP teams look at the overall structure of the school inclusive of teacher and student performance. Their observations help identify areas of strengths and those in need of growth. Composed of school leadership, teachers, staff members, and in many cases parent representatives, ScIP teams help school administrators make informed decisions on ways to improve the climate and culture of the school.

Another way to improve school climate and culture is through teacher-run social committees often called Sunshine Clubs. These committees are responsible for spearheading celebrations, acknowledging milestones, and promoting a sense of community among their members. To enhance the value of a school social committee, it is important for school leaders to allow teachers to take the lead. Teacher-driven social committees serve as the pulse of the building and can help boost both morale and productivity. Additionally, providing teachers with an opportunity to take on the responsibility of leading school-based social committees will help promote a school culture driven by teacher leadership. Such cultures thrive as successful leaders create opportunities for new leaders to emerge.

As an early childhood and primary school leader, you are a key factor in ensuring that students are provided with opportunities to succeed. Your goal is to intentionally cultivate an environment where learning is achieved through positive interactions and a focus on the whole child. You must develop relationships, provide your staff with feedback, and ensure that your school climate is one driven by positivity. Compliments are great motivators. During your daily rounds, make it a point to compliment children hard at work. Be intentional with what you say, and make sure you are mindful of the different learners, learning styles, and how they demonstrate learning. Don't forget about your teacher teams! They need compliments, too! Make sure you highlight good teaching and clever ideas. An email or brief intercom shout out can go a long way in motivating and boosting teacher and staff morale.

Leadership tip: Don't forget to use social media to tell your school's story! Principal Scott Passner is a highly motivated early childhood instructional leader who utilizes the Twitter hashtag #PisforPositive to promote an inclusive school culture. He often tweets about the amazing things going on in his building. His excitement for sharing the magic that happens in his early childhood center ignited his team's desire to share the magic as well. At any given point, Mr. Passner and his team of educators share their activities with the Twitterverse. Leverage technology to recognize your teams, your students, and to let the community know all the wonderful things happening in your building.

Tools to Use

Just as it is important to understand the needs of students, teachers, and staff it is equally important for school leaders to identify their own personal needs as well. Knowing your own strengths and weaknesses, as well as being mindful of what you need to successfully tend to the many tasks that will come your way will enhance your ability to seek the tools and resources that will facilitate your work as an instructional leader. There is a myriad of different tools leaders can use to facilitate their day-to-day school operations and interactions with students, teachers, staff members, and parents/caregivers. Below we have included a couple of tools that we have experienced and found to be critical to our work.

Calendars and Planners

Let's be real, there are not enough hours in the day to get through all the things that school leaders need to get through. However, you can be intentional with your time and create a plan of action to help you meet your goals. Using a calendar or a planner to distribute your daily, weekly, and monthly tasks is a surefire way to purposely manage your time. Calendars and planners can help you create schedules and allocate time for meetings, walkthroughs, feedback, etc. A word of caution: Be gentle with yourself. You can make a plan to tackle certain things but there is always the "unknown." Unknowns could be unexpected visitors, student concerns, or just the unexpected. Although you will be utilizing calendars and planners to maximize your time, you must still be flexible when the unexpected happens.

Now that we have identified calendars and planners as useful tools for instructional leaders let's briefly talk about the options. There are many styles to choose from. The layouts can be different depending on the purpose of your planning. Daily calendars and planners can help guide your day-to-day interactions and focused visibility. Weekly calendars provide you with a week-long layout that could help you to successfully plan for and structure your observations, walkthroughs, and meeting schedules. Monthly calendars can assist you in long-term planning and preparations such as family and community events or activities. If you prefer to use technology, you can create digital calendars and planners too. Google Calendar, Outlook Calendar, and web-based calendars are all great tools to utilize.

Video Recording and Conferencing Tools

School-wide engagement is an important aspect of an instructional leader's journey. Prior to the COVID-19 pandemic, we typically engaged students and the community through assemblies. However, the pandemic called for different ways through which instructional leaders could engage with students, teachers, and parents in a more efficient and socially distant way. Video recording and conferencing technology tools have transformed the way we engage school communities. We now have the potential to increase participation and attendance in our meetings and community events. Zoom, Microsoft Teams, and Webex have been critical in helping school leaders engage parents and caregivers. These technology tools should continue to be utilized to promote a sense of community, fortify relationships, and provide everyone with an opportunity to engage.

Digital Tools for Communication

The rise of the Internet has enabled schools in the United States to create school- and district-based web pages. These websites are serving as essential communication hubs for the dissemination of school information. In addition to school-based web pages, school leaders can leverage digital tools found in either Google Workspace or Microsoft Suite to generate newsletters containing school information. These newsletters could be placed on school websites for parents to access. There are also web-based applications that allow for the quick creation and distribution of newsletters containing school information to parents. Among these web applications are Smore newsletters, Blackboard Connect, and YouTube.

One dynamic school leader, Nicholas Edwards, has leveraged the Internet platform, YouTube, to share weekly updates with his school community. His videos are quick, relevant, and an easy way to keep all stakeholders informed. Considering the high population of Spanish-speaking parents within his school community, Principal Edwards ensures that the captions on his videos are provided in Spanish. He creates and disseminates one video per week creating a visual connection for his school community. Through his efforts, parents have remained connected and informed about all events and weekly happenings at their children's schools.

Tools for Assessing School Culture

Many tools are also available for you to audit, or conduct an official inspection of your school's culture, including the School Culture Triage Survey linked here: (https://connect.kasa.org/HigherLogic/System/DownloadDocumentFile.ashx?DocumentFileKey=b7f08b60-db15-4b5d-83c5-f00e2e99dc40). Be sure to adhere to your district's policies when administering any surveys with your faculty and staff to ensure that local guidelines, procedures, and protocols are followed.

It is important to find the right tools that can help facilitate your work. You want to work smarter and not harder. By learning how to navigate and use different tools, you will feel accomplished in your work as an early childhood and primary school leader.

Leadership tip: Try using a planner. Planners are magnificent tools as they can help you stay ahead of the game! Utilize the different sections of a planner: Daily, weekly, and monthly tasks. These sections will enhance your time management and planning skills to effectively handle all of your responsibilities and to-dos. Invite your school leadership team to help you gather ideas and plan for future activities. This action can help keep your administrative team on the same page as you all work toward improving school culture and achievement.

Celebrating Student Growth and Achievement

Celebrations are an important aspect of life. We celebrate birthdays, graduations, and marriages. When we celebrate and honor an occasion, those involved either directly or indirectly tend to exhibit feelings of happiness and joy. They also share a collective sense of belonging. With this mindset, school leaders must recognize the importance of celebrating their students. Students are motivated not only by their personal success but also by witnessing the success of their peers. This is essentially the basic premise of positive reinforcement. You observe a "good" behavior and then provide some form of praise or acknowledgment. This praise or acknowledgment serves as a way of reinforcing the student's actions and simultaneously captivating the attention of others who also want to receive a similar type of praise or acknowledgment.

There are endless possibilities for positive reinforcement. When promoting an environment driven by positive words, praise, and acknowledgment your students will undoubtedly emulate the behaviors that correlate to the building of a positive culture. In instances where students deviate from the norm, you will be able to redirect behaviors and lead students back on track. These instances will allow you to feel a great sense of accomplishment. Below, we have included a few of our favorite ways to build positive school cultures by celebrating and acknowledging student growth and achievements.

Morning Announcements
The morning announcement is a daily ritual in early childhood and primary school settings. Morning announcements are utilized to set the tone for the day. Typically, these announcements consist of a daily greeting or a positive affirmation. School leaders can be intentional about how they use the morning announcement. For example, highlighting student achievements and successes can help build excitement and pride for a job well done. Highlighting a student's or faculty member's birthday over the loudspeaker will certainly give our youngest learners something to be cheerful about. You

may also wish to give a shout out to a class or a particular student who has demonstrated kindness to others or perseverance in completing a difficult task. Your recognition will validate the student's action and get others thinking about how they can show kindness and persevere too. When planning for effective morning announcements, consider the following:

- **Keep your announcements short and sweet!** Try to limit your talking to three to four minutes tops! After all, the kids and teachers are eager and ready to start their day of learning! If there is anything you want to share that will take longer than three to four minutes, it is best to say it via email.
- **Focus on the positive!** Your morning announcements should always be positive and encouraging. Remember: They set the tone for the day! You want your students, teachers, and staff members to feel uplifted and inspired to tackle the day ahead.
- **Involve your students!** You can have teachers select students to recite the Pledge of Allegiance, the school mantra, or any other positive affirmation you come up with. Think about how excited students will be to get the opportunity to speak via the loud speaker!

Principal's Showcase Bulletin Board

We love a fun, interactive bulletin board; and guess what? Students love them too! It is no secret that students like to see their work displayed in their classrooms and outside of their rooms too. It helps build a collective sense of pride. Now imagine how students would feel if their work was celebrated by being displayed on the Principal's Showcase Bulletin Board?! We are not big on only showcasing immaculate work. Students struggle and work through the struggle to make sense of new content, difficult words, and abstract ideas. Acknowledging the work that goes into this productive struggle in learning can have a significant impact on students attempting to try new things in the future. Have a rotating schedule to display amazing student work outside of your office. Make it a BIG deal, take pictures, and praise students for their incredible work. Principal Bulletin Boards can help you build strong relationships with the students under your charge. They will provide you with conversation starters and will provide them with motivation to strive to do their best for the chance of being highlighted on the Principal's Bulletin Board.

Positive Principal Office Referrals

We must break away from the notion that students should only be sent to the principal's office if they have violated a rule and need to face disciplinary measures. The principal's office should be recognized as a safe zone too. Remember that as the building leader, you set the tone for your building. Turn your office into a space where students are rewarded for doing what is right, trying their best, or being a friend to someone in need. We suggest having a student-centered corner in your office. This corner should consist of children's books, sensory tools, rewards, and incentives ready for students to engage with. Designate a special time either weekly or monthly for students to be invited to your office by way of a Positive Principal Office Referral. This idea will help you build and strengthen your relationship with students. It will also allow students to view the principal's office in a positive way and not only when discipline issues arise.

Monthly School-Wide Convocations

It is important for students to understand that they are a part of a community of learners. As such, we advocate for monthly school-wide convocations. These do not have to be long dragged-out events. Rather, they should be short and concise. For example, we have used the character education traits as the focus of our monthly school-wide convocation. We began by telling our students the month's trait, along with its meaning, an example of how the trait could be practiced in school. We then acknowledged our school community by reciting our mantra, the monthly character trait, and finally by clapping for each other. This simple act created a unified sense of purpose within students, teachers, and staff. Monthly school-wide convocations can focus on character traits, positive affirmations, school mantras, and anything that will create a sense of unity and purpose for all.

Celebrations are critical to establishing a positive learning environment for your students, teachers, and staff members. Students in your school need to feel that you are constantly aware and involved in their successes. Providing students with opportunities in which their efforts and hard work are acknowledged and celebrated creates a sense of collective pride and joy within your school.

Eye on equity: Be mindful of the diverse learners in your school. Make a conscious effort to acknowledge and praise all students. Understand their needs and meet them where they are as learners. You must help cultivate learning environments that allow them to thrive. Ensuring that school is a place where they feel safe, cared for, and included is a great way to start. Expect them to be at different points of the learning journey but praise them all the same. Provide your teachers and grade-level teams opportunities to enhance their teaching repertoires through effective professional development that is conducive to the student population they serve. Give teachers opportunities to engage in teacher leadership. Be intentional about planning for opportunities to praise, validate, and guide all students. When you know, celebrate, and acknowledge your students, your teachers, and your staff you gain a deepened sense of accomplishment allowing you to create welcoming learning environments for all. Lastly, do not forget parents, caregivers, and community members. Provide them with opportunities to engage in school happenings and ensure transparency by providing timely communication and by ensuring said communication is conducive to the different languages found in your school setting.

Final Thoughts

This chapter focused on helping you establish a sense of accomplishment in the work that you do. Understanding that you need to get to know your students and the community they live in is part of leading the whole child. As an early childhood and primary school leader remember that your visibility matters. Your presence sets the tone for cultivating an environment where your students feel safe and included. Knowing your curriculum and understanding the different needs of your teaching teams will help you establish a course of action to ensure that learning is occurring because of effective teaching strategies and a student-centered approach.

Being mindful of the many tasks that come with the job, you must also be intentional about how you use your time. Maintaining a calendar to plan will help keep you on track. Leveraging technology and digital tools for communicating will also support you as you attempt to establish and solidify relationships. Finally, celebrating your students is non-negotiable. Your students need to understand that you value and acknowledge their efforts. When you reflect upon your leadership and the impact it is having not just on academics but also on your students' social and emotional well-being, you should begin to feel a sense of accomplishment. You are the leader your students and teachers need to excel.

Our Favorite Chapter Resource Links

- Smore Newsletters: https://www.smore.com
- https://workspace.google.com
- Microsoft Suite: Microsoft.com
- Blackboard Connect www.blackboard.com
- Zoom www.zoom.com
- Webexwww.webex.com
- Google Calendar www .Google.com

Chapter 6: Reflection Questions

- How am I managing my time efficiently?
- Are my students reflected in my school's curriculum?
- What am I doing to support my teachers to do the work that needs to be done?
- How am I communicating with parents, caretakers, and community partners?
- How frequently am I engaged with students?
- Am I familiar with my district's policies around the topics highlighted in this chapter?

Chapter 6: Spotting and Recognizing Student Engagement and Intentional Learning

Leadership Action Spotlight

Identify three takeaways from Chapter 6.

_____
_____
_____

Write down two ideas that you would like to implement in your current role.

OR for aspiring leaders

Write down two ideas that you would consider implementing in the future.

_____
_____
_____

Identify one lingering question or area you would like to explore further.

_____

_____

_____

Personal reflection, thoughts, comments, concerns, ideas:

_____

_____

_____

_____

Leading in Early Childhood Settings

Identifying Your Leadership Style

Purpose is essentially the reason why you choose to do the things that you do. It is your objective, your intention, your goal. To walk a meaningful path, you must identify and stay true to your purpose. Once you find your purpose, help cultivate purpose within others. Be the leader that you needed when you were trying to find your way. Know your purpose, live up to your purpose, and share your purpose with those around you.

****

Key Effective Characteristics of Early Childhood Leaders

Leadership is defined as the action of leading teams of individuals within institutions and organizations (Merriam-Webster, 2022). Early childhood and primary school leaders spearhead efforts to educate our youngest learners. As discussed in Chapter 1, the primary school years set the stage for future learning experiences leading up to successful adulthood. Due to the varying developmental needs and the immense diversity of young learners, you must embrace effective leadership qualities that will facilitate opportunities to propel students toward meeting and exceeding grade-level expectations. To help get you started, we share a few characteristics we have observed in successful early childhood and primary school leaders.

DOI: 10.4324/9781003219767-10

Lead with love: As an instructional leader, you need to be aware of the connection between leading with love and Maslow's hierarchy of needs. Recall the goal of the hierarchy is to get students to reach the point of self-actualization. This, however, can only occur once our children's basic physiological and safety needs are met. The next climb up the hierarchy requires students to feel loved and to develop a sense of belonging. These feelings help place students on the path of constructing, strengthening, and boosting their self-esteem, self-awareness, and self-love. Leaders who lead their students with love, kindness, and empathy are critical to students' development as they inch closer to the realization that they can accomplish their goals, do great things, and succeed in life.

Often, leaders are perceived as disciplinarians and rule-makers. While that is an important aspect of your job description, leading is not just about enforcing policies and discipline. Effective leaders spend time with their students. They learn their students' names, trade stories, and even share a joke or two. Leading with love calls for you to build and continuously work on fostering positive relationships with students. Your students must always be at the center of it all. When you lead with love you have the responsibility to accept and acknowledge your children just as they are. Your continuous efforts will cultivate a climate where students' diversities are seen as assets.

Leading with love is a leadership trait that will strengthen positive relationships with the people you lead. Effective early childhood leaders recognize that teachers are the heart of the school building. As such, you need to be present, visible, and actively monitoring the building's pulse to ensure the heart remains healthy and strong. Regular classroom visits and informal and formal walkthroughs will enhance your ability to identify your building's pulse. Reflect on what you hear, what you see, and what you feel. Acknowledge and praise the efforts. Provide support and encouragement when needed. Demonstrate kindness and lead by example. Your teams are there to do the best they can for students. Echo their efforts by being involved. Consider the amount of time you spend behind your desk versus the amount of time you devote to visiting teachers and students. Provide your teams with opportunities to seek guidance and support when they need it. Give frequent, actionable, and positive feedback that will result in increased teacher efficacy. Respect your teachers' autonomy. Facilitate opportunities to engage in collaboration. Leading with love requires you to be present and visible. Your visibility and engagement as an instructional leader will set the tone for a culture driven by mutual respect, understanding, and the collective goal of providing students with positive learning experiences. Leading your staff with love, kindness, and empathy will facilitate the valiant effort of ensuring that students obtain the necessary guidance and support needed to be successful.

Flexible and patient: While at a yoga and meditation class I heard one of the instructors say, "We bend our bodies so that we don't break and instead gain flexibility in our flow." The idea suggested that if we are not flexible and patient with our intentions, our efforts, and the overall process of bending our bodies we will inadvertently bend to the point of breaking. We saw this anecdote personified in some of the effective leaders we have encountered throughout our combined journey in education. Those leaders understood that things will not happen overnight, that change and learning take time, that building positive relationships requires work, and that flexibility and patience are essential components to leading effective instructional teams.

When speaking about flexibility and patience in leadership, we are not indicating you need to forgo all deadlines! Effective leaders understand the necessity for timelines and are mindful of the many efforts, resources, tools, and time that are necessary to achieve the desired goal. When considering your students, you must be guided by the fact that they are inherently different, that they blossom at different times, and that they require different levels of support to be successful. Having a grasp on the stages of development along with understanding evolving learning and development theories will guide you in making decisions that are conducive to your students' needs.

Similarly, successfully leading a group of diverse teachers and staff also requires flexibility and patience. You will find yourself leading teachers who are at different points in their careers. At any given time, you may find yourself leading instructional teams consisting of veteran teachers, new teachers, highly effective teachers, and teachers in need of additional support. As the instructional leader, you must execute flexibility and patience as teachers try new ideas, ask for support, and seek opportunities to grow professionally. The keys to harvesting the power of flexibility and patience with the adults in your building without running the risk of chaos are feedback and visibility. Make sure that you are consistently and frequently providing your teacher teams with actionable, timely, and relevant feedback. Your feedback will help lead teachers in the direction that best supports students. Once again, your visibility and engagement with teachers and staff will set the tone, help motivate, and empower your teacher teams. Knowing that your leadership is driven by love, your teachers may even take instructional risks and invite you to observe. When this happens, know that your actions have empowered teachers to think outside the box as they put students first.

Empathetic: Empathy is characterized as the ability to see things in other people's perspectives. Empathetic leaders understand that while they are responsible for making instructional and organizational decisions, those decisions have an impact on students, teachers, staff, parents, and caregivers too. Therefore, it is important for you to step out of your leadership shoes and attempt to see things in other stakeholders' perspectives. Consider the following questions:

- *How are your decisions affecting students?*
- *How are your decisions impacting teachers and staff?*
- *How will parents and caregivers perceive your decisions?*

Empathy will drive you to consider all angles and allow you to make better decisions. One important suggestion or idea that you must come to terms with early on in your leadership journey is the fact that your decisions will not always make every single stakeholder group happy. With this in mind, remember that students must always be at the center of the decision-making process. All of your decisions must be driven by the notion that they will help improve student outcomes.

Aside from the decision-making process, leaders must demonstrate empathy when engaging with students, teachers, staff, parents, and caregivers. Empathetic leaders listen intently. They acknowledge other people's feelings, questions, or concerns. This, however, does not indicate that empathetic leaders make decisions based on other constituents' feelings and perspectives. As the instructional leader of your building, you must also learn that you can be empathetic yet firm. For example, you may encounter a concerned parent who expresses her perspectives on student discipline. While you may show empathy by listening attentively and putting yourself in the parents' perspectives, doing so may not change the outcome. You must be comfortable with showing empathy while remaining firm in upholding decisions that were made in the best interest of students. You may not make everyone happy, but you maintained open lines of communication, demonstrated empathy, and made decisions based on students. On a side note, during these types of situations, do not take things personally. Know that if your decisions were made based on the needs of your students and with the goal of guiding and supporting them, you have made the right decision. Students must always be at the center of the decision-making process.

Influencers: With the help of social media, the term influencer has truly transformed individuals and institutions. After much consideration and thought, we like to suggest that instructional leaders are influencers, too. By definition an influencer is someone who inspires and motivates others. Inspiration and motivation are at the heart of instructional leadership. Effective early childhood and primary school leaders are tasked with motivating and influencing every aspect of the school day. From the morning announcement, to instructional walkthroughs, to chats with students during recess, your role is to be visible. Your visibility will influence outcomes!

If your leadership has influenced and resulted in an engaging and inspiring school climate, chances are everyone will hear about it! As an influencer, you must also take part in the sharing of good news. In Chapter 2 we spoke about ways to cultivate caring environments. We highlighted a few social media platforms like Instagram and Twitter as platforms that could help elevate your school's status by shedding a positive light on all of your school's happenings. You want the opportunity to share the good news! You want to influence and motivate all stakeholders to view your school as the amazing learning zone it is. Do not forget that pictures are worth a thousand words. Leverage social media to share actual footage of the greatness in your building. Consistent effort is crucial, and top-notch influencer status is not achieved overnight. Keep engaging, keep motivating, keep influencing the elements that will help shape and move your student outcomes.

It is important to understand that a large part of your role as an early childhood and primary school leader is to build, enhance, and sustain positive relationships that help you cultivate engaging and thriving learning environments. As the leader, you must be much more than the decision-maker. To effectively lead, consider how you will demonstrate empathy, patience, flexibility, and love to influence stakeholder engagement, growth, and development.

Leadership Styles

There are various leadership styles that are reflective of the leader's personality, core values, and purpose. As new or aspiring early childhood leaders, you must carefully consider the type of leader you want to be. Prior to this, however, you should take some time to reflect and identify your leadership purpose. When attempting to identify your leadership purpose, consider the following questions:

- What are my core leadership values?
- What type of leader do I want to be?

- How do I support others?
- In what ways do I motivate and inspire others?
- How do I show appreciation?
- Am I approachable?
- How do I recognize an individual's hard work and efforts?
- Are positive relationships crucial to me and the work I do?
- Is the way people feel when I am around important to me?
- What kind of legacy do I want to leave behind?

Knowing your leadership purpose will place you on the path of working toward becoming the best leader you possibly can be for those individuals you lead. Your purpose sets the tone for your leadership style: *Will you micromanage your teams? Will you give them a certain degree of autonomy?* Your leadership style sets the tone for the culture of your school: *Will you inspire trust? Will you facilitate innovation?* It is imperative that you consider your leadership purpose to identify your leadership style.

We have included a description of the most popular leadership styles possessed by some of the leaders we have encountered throughout our collective leadership journey. While this is not an exhaustive list of styles, the following descriptions along with the reflection questions included above should facilitate your thinking and guide you toward identifying your personal leadership style.

Transactional Leadership

Transactional leadership is a style of leadership driven by compliance, order, and structure. This type of leadership has a clearly defined hierarchy in which leaders look for compliance or results from their subordinates. In this dichotomy, subordinates who do not adhere to the mandates, protocols, or procedures are often reprimanded. Transactional leaders prioritize the chain of command and closely monitor their subordinates. They are goal-oriented and tend to use rewards as motivators for the attainment of specific goals (Howell and Avolio, 1993). While it can be beneficial to establish and follow a chain of command in organizations with multiple leaders, transactional leadership can have its drawbacks in education. The close monitoring of staff for example can take away from the teachers' and staff members' autonomy, limiting creativity and motivation. Such effects tend to permeate the status quo mentality thus inhibiting innovation.

Distributive or Shared Leadership

Distributive leadership is also referred to as shared leadership or shared management. This leadership style is conducive to organizations that have multiple individuals holding leadership positions. Although there may be a hierarchy such as building principal and assistant principal, distributive leadership is grounded upon the notion that leadership responsibilities are to be distributed among the members of the leadership team. Camburn et al. (2003) suggested that leaders who utilize a distributive leadership style share the responsibility across different people and different situations. Klar (2012) described this form of leadership as one that is conducive to collaboration among the different leaders in an organization. Mitgang et al. (2013), indicated that in schools, distributive leadership enhances the effectiveness of the school leader as it enables the leader to leverage the strengths of individual members to complete tasks and collectively work to reach a common goal. While it can be an advantageous leadership style, distributive leadership has its disadvantages. For example, communication and collaboration between the leadership team must be prioritized. Distributive leadership is not the delegation of tasks as in the case of transactional leadership. Leaders who simply delegate tasks can find themselves far removed from important information, curricular changes, or innovation that may otherwise help grow their team's collective efficacy. A breakdown in communication and collaboration can hinder the collaborative nature of distributive leadership.

Servant Leadership

A servant leadership style is characterized by leaders who see themselves as individuals with the opportunity to serve their followers. These leaders often share responsibilities and invite followers to share their perspectives, ideas, and solutions while attempting to solve problems. Servant leaders are often good listeners who want opportunities to understand and tend to the needs of the people they serve. Their goal is to help their followers grow and develop professionally. Servant leaders help cultivate environments driven by trust, respect, and admiration. As such, they emphasize and promote the idea that mistakes are opportunities to learn. They often engage in the act of uplifting their staff members through positive affirmations and an "all hands on deck" approach. According to the Center for Creative Leadership (2021), there are four tenets to the servant leadership style. These include sharing the power, putting the needs of others before your own, helping others grow and develop, and collaborating for the greater good. While servant leadership is characterized by these positive attributes, a challenge to servant leadership is a perceived lack of authority as the role of the leader is diminished. A perceived lack of authority can cause potential problems for productivity and can result in the breakdown of accountability.

Transformational Leadership

John Maxwell once said, "leaders become great not because of their power, but because of their ability to empower others." This is the premise of transformational leadership, a leadership style characterized by leaders who want to inspire and motivate their teams. Transformational leaders are visionaries who embrace growth mindsets and the challenges brought upon by change. They understand the value of relationships and take great pride in guiding, supporting, and empowering their teams. They are key players in creating positive school cultures and climates built around a collective vision. They utilize this shared vision and mission to motivate and encourage their employees to meet and exceed expectations (Leithwood et al., 1996). Bass (1997) suggested that transformational leaders establish and maintain positive relationships among employees. In school settings, transformational leadership can be challenged by those who have adopted a status quo mentality. Transformational leadership requires long-term planning.

Instructional Leadership

Instructional leadership is characterized by leaders who view themselves as role models and elect to work alongside their teaching teams. They provide instructional support and guidance to ensure there is a focus on the best teaching practices that will help increase student achievement. Instructional leaders are lifelong learners who look for ways to stay abreast on issues impacting their schools, students, teachers, teaching, and learning. Jenkins (2009) suggested that instructional leaders must have a visible presence in the school and within classrooms. These leaders do not shy away from opportunities to jump into modeling and facilitating classroom instruction. They promote collaboration across and within grade levels and are interested in listening to and supporting their teachers. Providing their teachers with effective professional development opportunities is important to instructional leaders as they want to increase teacher capacity and efficacy.

What Is the Best Leadership Style?

We have provided you with a description of five common leadership styles we have observed of early childhood leaders during our collective journey in education. In our humble opinion, the best leaders we have encountered have unique leadership styles because they elected to deploy the use of a combination of the characteristics found in the leadership styles described above. For example, Ms. Dora Cavallo, an elementary school principal, is an exceptional instructional leader whose leadership style embodies a combination of characteristics derived from instructional, transformational, servant, and distributive leadership. Her leadership purpose is always grounded in motivating and empowering her teachers and grade-level teams to work hard to raise student achievement. She believes in teacher leadership and allows her teachers to make instructional decisions that help engage their students. Principal Cavallo utilizes all available resources to cultivate a warm, caring, inspiring, and student-centered culture. She is often seen visiting classrooms, interacting with students, engaged with teachers, and visibly involved with parents and caretakers as they drop students off in the morning. Principal Cavallo is an eager participant in school-wide activities leading a culture of inclusivity, tolerance, and an overwhelming sense of belonging. She leads with intention, consistency, fairness, and love.

The best leadership style for YOU is the one that best reflects your personality, your leadership purpose, and the vision of your school setting. Remember, you do not need to fit into any one particular leadership style. To identify your leadership style, reflect upon the questions included at the beginning of this chapter. Identify your leadership purpose. Decide on the type of culture you want to lead. If it helps, think back on your favorite manager, boss, or leader. What was it about this individual that stood out in your mind? How did this person lead? How did you feel around this individual? These are all important questions to consider when attempting to formulate your personal leadership style.

Eye of equity: Leaders must always lead with purpose. For the most part, a leadership purpose encompasses the need for schools to offer all students the ability to work to their full potential. This also means that aside from having a leadership purpose, leaders must lead with equity in mind. Whatever leadership style (or combination) you feel compelled to adopt, know that you must continue to focus on creating learning environments that are culturally relevant and conducive to the needs of the diverse student populations in your school. Lead through an equity lens. Maintain and promote high expectations for all. Challenge status quo mentalities by promoting solution-driven discussions to help mitigate issues of inequities. Focus your leadership efforts on building and sustaining a culture of inclusivity.

Final Thoughts

This chapter focused on summarizing characteristics observed in effective early childhood and primary school leaders. We suggested that in order to build positive relations conducive to a positive school culture, leaders should lead with love. Leaders must be flexible and patient as they drive teams to focus on meeting the needs of the students. They must understand that differentiation for both the students and the adults they lead is an essential component of leading. This leads to the idea that leaders must demonstrate the ability to show empathy. Empathy provides leaders with a deeper understanding as to why things may be happening and allows them to think of their constituents' needs when attempting to come up with solutions to guide and support teaching and learning. Finally, we suggested that early childhood and primary school leaders must be influencers within their school community. They must understand that excitement breeds excitement. To be a positive influence within the school community, leaders must be visible.

To lead effectively, you must lead with purpose. Leading with purpose implies that you have a vision for what your school should feel like and how you will choose to lead. While there are various leadership styles, the style you decide to adopt should be a reflection of your personality, your goals, and your vision. When trying to identify the style that best suits you, know that you are not tied down to just one style of leadership. Many highly effective leaders adopt characteristics from various leadership styles. Ultimately, your leadership style will help cultivate a caring school culture, driven by motivated and empowered educators who work their magic to meet the needs of the students.

Chapter 7: Reflection Questions

- What type of relationship do I want to have with my leadership team?
- How will I distribute the workload?
- Will I be guided by individual strengths or interests?
- How will I involve my team in the decision-making process?
- How will I hold others accountable?
- How will I enable opportunities for teacher leadership? Sharing ideas?

Chapter 7: Identifying Your Leadership Style

Leadership Action Spotlight

Identify three takeaways from Chapter 7.

_____

_____

_____

Write down two ideas that you would like to implement in your current role.

OR for aspiring leaders

Write down two ideas that you would consider implementing in the future.

_____

_____

_____

Identify one lingering question or area you would like to explore further.

_____

_____

_____

Personal reflection, thoughts, comments, concerns, ideas:

_____

_____

_____

_____

_____

Refining Our Leadership Approach through Culturally Responsive Teaching

Positive Affirmation: I Am Intentional about Cultivating an Inclusive Culture

Each day, your students arrive at school carrying personal experiences that form how they see the world around them. Their worldview is impacted by culture, language, ethnicity, socioeconomic status, and a myriad of other environmental factors. Some of your students may arrive with trauma resulting from unmet needs, struggle, or neglect. As the instructional leader, aim to create a learning environment where all students experience, feel, and understand that they matter. Building an inclusive culture requires your commitment to being intentional and consistent in providing equitable learning opportunities for all.

****

What Is Culturally Responsive Teaching?

Culturally responsive teaching is a research-based approach that encourages the connection of students' life experiences, cultures, and languages. When we consider how to teach and engage the whole child, as suggested in Chapter 3, we must always take into account children's experiences as they are a part of who these students are. Their lived experiences are relevant to their ability to engage in and motivation for learning. Leaders who recognize, understand, and are intentional about meeting students where and how they are, cultivate safe learning environments where students feel

DOI: 10.4324/9781003219767-11

respected, recognized, and included. Their actions result in the creation of a collective sense of belonging within the school community.

In Chapter 1, we introduced Maslow's hierarchy of needs and discussed the fact that basic needs must be met before students can begin working toward reaching self-actualization. When we think of the students in our classrooms, schools, and districts we have to consider Maslow's hierarchy of needs as an essential theory for learning and development. One question that every instructional leader should frequently revisit is "How are my actions, initiatives, and interactions helping my students feel included?" Instructional leaders should reflect on this question monthly if not on a weekly basis. Intentional efforts to foster a sense of belonging are crucial for the success of students in any age group, grade level, or district. It is imperative that students are able to establish a sense of belonging to and within a school community for them to develop esteem for themselves and those around them. Ensuring that learning institutions are conducive to meeting children's basic needs will enable students to look forward to coming to school, to engage in school activities, and to be motivated to work up to their potential.

To be intentional and consistent about creating learning environments that embrace the cultural wealth and diversity of your students you must think, act, and reflect with a culturally responsive mindset. Use the following questions to springboard your actions and planning:

- How are you empowering your students?
- How do you ensure that their voices are reflected in the school experience?
- Have you established school-wide activities that affirm student diversity while supporting a collective sense of belonging?
- How are you including your community when planning these school-wide events?
- How are your teachers and grade-level teams creating lessons that build confidence and self-awareness?
- How are you ensuring that diversity, inclusivity, and equity are at the forefront of the decision-making process?

These are important questions to reflect on when working, thinking, planning, and executing educational programming through a culturally responsive mindset. It is not just a one-time event, and you cannot be a one-trick pony. Being culturally responsive is a commitment to the students you serve. It requires you to get to know them as the little persons they are with the goal of helping them transform into the adults they are destined to be. To achieve this, you must view students as assets to you, your school, and the community. Believe in their potential, honor their identities, and let them know every day just how much they matter.

Eye on equity: You may encounter colleagues, teachers, and staff members who are quick to point out deficiencies in students. For example, you may hear "Those students just can't …" or "They just don't get it." We challenge you to eradicate this type of deficit view of students. Equity instruction means that everyone is on board with finding ways to scaffold, guide, and support students as they meet challenging concepts. Tailoring instruction to meet the needs of students is a crucial component of equity in instruction. As the instructional leader, consider leading the efforts to ensure that your teachers and staff members are actively seeking ways to support students. Keep abreast of new teaching strategies and professional development opportunities that can help you lead the efforts in building a school-wide culturally responsive growth mindset. Deficit mindsets have no place in the classroom.

Leadership tip: A school-wide pledge is a great way to recognize your school community's diversity by affirming the greatness embodied by the students you serve. Gather a committee of students, parents/caregivers, teachers, and staff and create a school pledge. Invite the school to recite the pledge daily during morning announcements. In Chapter 4, we advocate for social and emotional learning (SEL) to be at the forefront of the school community. SEL and culturally responsive teaching work hand in hand! Consider hosting a school-wide read aloud of *All Because You Matter* by Tami Charles. Find out what matters to students in your school. Find out what matters to your teachers, too! Posing open-ended questions, such as "I wish this school had …" can lead to helpful insights about what children and adults in your community long for and care about.

Affirming Young Children's Identities through Culturally Responsive Teaching

Having a culturally responsive mindset is the first step in establishing an inclusive learning environment. The next step is ensuring that everyone understands the importance of affirming students' identities and diverse experiences as assets when it comes to delivering and enhancing the district or school-approved curriculum. It is imperative that school leaders promote the notion that the curriculum is merely the vehicle or method utilized to teach students the standards they need to achieve to be successful in their respective grade levels. Operating with a culturally responsive mindset through an equity lens, guide your teachers and grade-level teams to tailor, scaffold, and provide children with the tools, resources, and strategies they need to be successful. Early childhood leaders can achieve this goal through school-wide culturally responsive literacy practices that are beneficial to all students. When observing culturally responsive early childhood and primary school settings, we have noted the following characteristics as catalysts for culturally responsive learning environments:

> **Positive mindset:** Having a positive mindset indicates that you, your teachers, and grade-level teams believe in all students' potential to learn, achieve, and be successful. This mindset correlates with having high expectations. When school leaders believe that their students can achieve greatness, they lead in a manner that facilitates greatness! When teachers believe that their students can achieve greatness, they teach in a manner that facilitates greatness! Keep a positive mindset when guiding your teachers and grade-level teams.

> Maintaining the same positive attitude when referencing and engaging with parents, caregivers, and the community will help improve your relationships. Similar to your students, you must do away with viewing parents through a deficit lens. If there are barriers with communication, eliminate them by having translators. If timing and location are the issue, allow for different times, days, and methods of communication. If motivation is an area of concern, elicit participation by offering incentives, raffles, or serving light refreshments. Your leadership team, teachers, and staff can help you brainstorm ideas to eliminate barriers that limit parent engagement in school functions. Set the tone of having high expectations for parents and caregivers to be actively involved at the beginning of the school year. If negativity arises, challenge it and instead invite the sharing of solutions. Whatever you do, remember the following:

> *As the leader, you set the tone.*
> *Have a positive mindset and drive high expectations.*

> **Leadership tip:** A positive mindset can often be confused with toxic positivity, or the belief that folks should maintain a positive attitude regardless of the challenges or difficult circumstances one faces. On the other hand, these beliefs when combined with a growth mindset can charge a school

community to realize: "We're not there … yet, but we can consider solutions to our challenges." Regardless of how you frame having high expectations for all learners, know that store-bought posters and terminology will only get you so far as a leader. Commit to the real work of designing opportunities that allow all students to achieve while increasing opportunities for parents and caregivers to be involved in their children's educational journey. Celebrate those successes, no matter how big or small.

Engagement: Schools and classrooms working with a culturally responsive mindset consider engagement as a crucial component to learning. Engagement in culturally responsive classrooms acknowledges and embraces students as they are. This is evidenced by teachers who facilitate learning opportunities where students make discoveries and collaborate with one another to solve and respond to essential questions. Consequently, students play an active role in forming discussions and using their resources, backgrounds, and experiences to create, affirm, and expand their worldviews. This will of course look different from classroom to classroom. Allowing opportunities for students to engage in inquiry, work through struggles, and collaborate with peers enhances opportunities for students to be actively engaged instead of being passive listeners.

Effective early childhood leaders must also promote active engagement with teachers, staff, and students alike. This can be achieved through school-wide assemblies or weekly convocations. As the instructional leader, you must find ways to model what culturally responsive and equity-driven engagement looks like. Consider the morning announcement for instance, how exciting would it be to give the opportunity to recite the pledge of allegiance to one of your quiet, introverted, English learners? Do you think it will help boost the child's self-esteem? Do you think it will help support an inclusive community? Do you think it will help generate other opportunities for all students to engage? Equity work helps to eradicate barriers and maximizes potential. Whatever strategy you choose to deploy, remember the following:

As the leader, you set the tone.

Build community through school-wide engagement opportunities.

Curriculum access: Students have a right to access a curriculum that is relevant, timely, and diverse. Curricular diversity references the idea that the school curriculum is inclusive of gender, race, ethnicity, abilities, disabilities, language, culture, etc. Ensuring that students have access to a curriculum that is both robust and diverse takes careful planning, preparation, and an equity lens.

It is important to differentiate the terms equity and equality when having discussions about making the curriculum accessible. Equality implies equal access to the curriculum. By definition, it means that "all students" are provided the "same" level of support to access and meet the grade-level standards taught through the curriculum. Equity refers to providing fair access to the curriculum. This definition suggests that "each student" is to be provided with the appropriate level of "differentiated scaffolding and support" that he or she needs to successfully meet the grade-level standards taught through the curriculum.

In other words, we must not look at students with a "one-size-fits-all" mentality. To ensure appropriate, equity-driven access to the district's curriculum, leaders, teachers, and grade-level teams must ensure that differentiated levels of support are in place to meet the needs of their diverse student populations.

When you operate with a culturally responsive mindset that is focused on ensuring equity of instruction you make every effort to guarantee that students are provided with whatever it is they need to meet the grade-level standards taught through the district's curriculum. Many states have begun to adopt statewide mandates when it comes to diversity in the curriculum, as well. At the time of this book's publication, for example, New Jersey legislated curriculum in K–12 settings to include economic diversity, equity, inclusion, tolerance, and belonging in connection with (1) gender and sexual orientation, (2) race and ethnicity, (3) disabilities, and (4) religious tolerance. Added to the legislation at the time of writing this book is the inclusion of Asian American and Pacific Islander (AAPI) representation in curriculum. As you consider your school's curriculum in relation to your students and their needs, remember the following:

As the leader, you set the tone.

Equity-driven instructional practices provide students with the tools they need to effectively meet the grade-level standards taught through the district's curriculum.

Eye on equity: The curriculum consists of the tools and resources educators utilize to teach students the standards. When guiding your teachers and grade-level teams, have discussions around inclusivity. Ensure that classroom libraries have inclusive books and that teachers incorporate diversity into their read alouds and lesson plans. It is important for students to see themselves in some of the stories they hear and read. Give them the flexibility of choice by allowing them to select their own books to read during independent reading time. Celebrate their choices and harvest a love for learning.

Leadership tip: Become familiar with your ever-evolving local and state curriculum mandates. These changes will often impact early childhood settings and may require parent and community outreach and/or specialized training of faculty and staff.

Inclusivity: Building community and fostering inclusivity are non-negotiable when it comes to leading and teaching with a culturally responsive mindset. Students must acquire a sense of belonging to begin feeling like a part of the classroom community. School leaders, teachers, and staff play an important role in establishing inclusive practices. Teachers, for example, can make gains toward creating inclusive environments by getting to know each of their students. Asking them about their lives, the types of things they enjoy, the types of things they dislike can all contribute to the building of inclusivity. As a leader, you can ensure that inclusive practices are driving forces behind student recognitions and school-wide celebrations. Celebrate diversity by showcasing different cultures and languages. Incorporate the practice of kindness, empathy, and love. Demonstrate genuine care and concern for all, and acknowledge the differences that make us unique. Respect and establish trusting relationships. In time, mutual respect and acceptance will be the driving force of your school's culture. However you choose to establish inclusive practices in your school, please remember the following:

As the leader, you set the tone.

Inclusive practices promote trust, establish relationships, and foster a culture of acceptance.

Access to Books and Inclusive Materials

The use of inclusive books and materials is crucial to fostering a sense of belonging in children's respective classrooms and schools. Inclusive and culturally responsive resources help bridge the equity gap and aid in promoting self-awareness, confidence, and resiliency in students. As a leader in education, the International Literacy Association's (2018) Children's Rights to Read includes a call for books that serve as windows, mirrors, and open doors into the diverse lives and experiences of others. Based on the work of Rudine Sims Bishop, this belief ensures that students see themselves in the curriculum, develop empathy for others, and build background knowledge. The interview linked below is featured in Reading Rockets and provides an excellent introduction to the concept of viewing books as windows, mirrors, and doors: https://www.readingrockets.org/teaching/experts/rudine -sims-bishop.

Consider the following scenario: An administrative team is notified that a small, but significant amount of federal grant money will be allocated to ensure that immigrant students and their families engage in meaningful and authentic literacy experiences. While no materials were readily available, the team met to design "Bienvenidos Book Club," a K–3 program for immigrant students and their families. After looking at data regarding students' countries of origin and languages spoken at home, six themes were developed across the program and mentor texts were selected to reflect students and their unique cultural experiences. Soon, Bienvenidos Book Club was born, paving the way for families who wanted opportunities to engage in learning alongside their children.

Instead of imagining this scenario as a "nice-to-have" option, make it a priority in your work as an early childhood leader. Determine what funds are available or needed. To ensure inclusivity, you must continuously advocate for the different populations in your school community. Leverage your resources, call upon community members, and engage the input of parents and caregivers as a collective effort to facilitate the success of implementing inclusive practices in your school. For example, in the scenario above, parents participated in a roundtable discussion. This discussion led the administrative team to realize that parents were interested and willing to hone their linguistic skills and ability to speak English alongside their children. Hence, Bienvenidos Book Club was born!

Leadership tip: In *Literacy Changemakers: Bringing the Joy of Reading and Writing into Focus for Teachers and Students* (2020), Kunz, Hall, and Lella share a checklist for ensuring that classroom libraries and book access in school communities are interdisciplinary and inclusive in nature. Use tools like these to self-assess what materials are readily available, or not, in your school community. Ensure that access to diverse texts and materials reflects current state and local curriculum mandates. Also, consider whether or not all children in the community have access to materials that address the spirit of Children's Rights to Read.

Enhancing Curriculum: Not Just Relying on "Programs"

While many of the examples shared in this chapter are authentic solutions to designing and implementing culturally responsive teaching, it goes without saying that education is a business that is flooded by many commercial "solutions" to local challenges. Many of these materials and resources have been reviewed by the What Works Clearinghouse (https://ies.ed.gov/ncee/wwc/), but many also leave early childhood leaders left to determine where to seek resources. We share in our colleagues' beliefs that there is no silver-bullet when it comes to ensuring that the needs of young learners are met. In fact, many research studies highlight that access, time, and beliefs matter more. Students need access to quality resources and materials. They need time to flourish in environments that are supportive, culturally relevant, and affirming. They need teachers who believe in them so that they, too, can identify with the mantra: "This teacher believes in me and has my best interests at heart." Are there good packaged materials and programs out there to support learners? Absolutely! However, it is our belief that finding your "why" has to come before finding the "what." Live and walk in your purpose. Leverage available resources to guide and support the work of educating, advocating, and supporting children to achieve academic, social, and emotional success while learning how to navigate the world around them.

Eye on equity: When reflecting on your school's curricular programs, remember the notion that they will not be one-size-fits-all. Careful preparation and planning must be ongoing to breathe life into curricular programs. Strategies like identifying effective scaffolding, remediating, and extending teaching practices will help teachers and instructional leaders engage in the deployment of strategies that enhance learning for all students.

Final Thoughts

This chapter defined culturally responsive teaching as a research-based approach that encourages the connection of students' life experiences, cultures, and languages. Culturally responsive teaching matters in all school settings. This approach helps to affirm students' identities as learners. Instructional leaders set the tone for inclusivity and culturally responsive schools. They lead with positive mindsets, they advocate for increased inclusive engagement practices, and they advocate for a curriculum that is taught in ways that ensure the success of all students. One way instructional leaders pave the way for inclusive teaching practices that value, promote, and enhance the diversity of students is through books. Early childhood settings should contain access to books that are reflective of the students who attend the school. Curriculum programs should not be taken as one-size-fits-all opportunities to learn. In contrast, the curriculum must be critically analyzed, structured, and enhanced in ways that could help build upon students' learning experiences.

Our Favorite Chapter Resource Links

- Step into ESL LitCamp: https://edublog.scholastic.com/post/shared-literacy-community-values-step-esl-litcamp
- What Works Clearinghouse: https://ies.ed.gov/ncee/wwc/
- Culturally Responsive Teaching and the Brain: https://www.google.com/books/edition/Culturally_Responsive_Teaching_and_The_B/BxGoBQAAQBAJ?hl=en&gbpv=1&dq=culturally+responsive+teaching&printsec=frontcover
- Cultivating Genius: https://www.google.com/books/edition/Cultivating_Genius/8M5hyAEACAAJ?hl=en
- Culturally Relevant Pedagogy: Asking a Different Question https://www.amazon.com/Culturally-Relevant-Pedagogy-Sustaining-Pedagogies/dp/0807765910/ref=sr_1_2?keywords=9780807765913&linkCode=qs&qid=1645489182&s=books&sr=1-2

Chapter 8: Reflection Questions

- Based on the chapter, consider how well you know your students.
- Do you invite and involve families in inclusive ways?
- How are students' identities respected, cultivated, and developed across the curriculum?
- Are first languages and bilingual learners celebrated for their cultural assets?
- Are spaces designed to include conversations with teachers around culturally responsive teaching as they enhance their practice?

Chapter 8: Redefining Our Leadership Approach through Culturally Responsive Teaching

Leadership Action Spotlight

Identify three takeaways from Chapter 8.

_____

_____

_____

Write down two ideas that you would like to implement in your current role.

OR for aspiring leaders

Write down two ideas that you would consider implementing in the future.

_____

_____

_____

Identify one lingering question or area you would like to explore further.

_____

_____

_____

Personal reflection, thoughts, comments, concerns, ideas:

_____

_____

_____

_____

_____

Failing Forward as an Early Childhood Changemaker

9

Wouldn't it be great if all our attempts at new challenges resulted in successes? Unfortunately, that is not always the case. Facing anything new requires a learning curve and time to step back to reflect before attempting to try again. Mistakes provide us with opportunities to start over. They are undeniable proof of our resilience, perseverance, and fervent efforts to succeed. Do not dwell on your mistakes. Reflect, refocus, and keep on working toward achieving success.

Breathe in the Reflection, Exhale Your Affection

Serving in a leadership role is difficult. You encounter different personalities each with their respective likes and dislikes. As a decision-maker, you are bound to make decisions that impact others, and those decisions may not always be well received. Sometimes you may even face resistance and push back. Other times, your choices may not work out as planned. In each of these instances, consider your actions and reflect on their results.

Reflection is an integral part of the leadership process. It is also a key effective practice in the realm of teaching too! This is because reflection allows you to look deep into your core and explore the reasons behind your decision making. When you reflect, you intentionally think about your values, skills, and dispositions. You can identify the reasons behind your decisions and take corrective steps toward ensuring that future actions yield favorable results. One important aspect of reflection is realizing that every

DOI: 10.4324/9781003219767-12

mistake or unfavorable decision is providing you with an opportunity to learn. Reflecting and adjusting are part of the process.

In educational leadership, we often hear the phrase *reflective leadership*. What exactly constitutes a reflective leadership style? Does it simply involve the act of reflection? One of our favorite definitions of the term reflective leadership is derived from Sara Horton-Deutsch. Horton-Deutsch (2013) defined reflective leadership as follows:

> a way of approaching the work of being a leader by leading one's life with presence and personal mastery. Learning to be present, to be aware and attentive to our experience with people throughout the day is the focus of reflective leadership.

In Chapter 4 we discussed characteristics we have observed in effective early childhood and primary school leaders. Those consisted of leading with love, being flexible, patient, demonstrating empathy, and becoming influencers in their school community. If we compare our observations with Horton-Deutsch's definition of reflective leadership, we can identify several similarities. For one, reflective leadership requires a degree of awareness and attentiveness. Effective leaders do just that! They are visible throughout the school day and are frequently spotted visiting classrooms and interacting with students, teachers, and staff.

Through the practice of reflective leadership, leaders can be guided toward making instructional decisions for the benefit of students, teachers, and staff they serve. When decisions do not go as planned, reflective leaders are able to utilize their observations in conjunction with their daily experiences to reflect and adjust accordingly. Reflection is a prerequisite for leading with love. Having an awareness of your vision, mission, and desired outcomes will help you to continue to make the best decision possible for your schools.

However, there is one caveat: Your decisions will not always make everyone happy. There will be many times in which you will face the heat of having to deal with an unhappy teacher, staff member, parent, caregiver, etc. When this occurs, demonstrate empathy, allow individuals to express their concerns or frustrations, and express awareness of your decisions and why. Always reflect on your interactions with unhappy constituents. Consider possible outcomes and be firm about your decisions, honest about your intentions, and empathetic to the other party's concerns. Chances are that all they wanted was to be acknowledged and heard. Remember, you set the tone; reflect on your interactions. Consider how you could have been more accessible or a better listener.

Reflective leadership takes patience and time to develop. Keep in mind that when you reflect, you think about where you are as a leader. You consider your actions, your thoughts, your decisions, and the outcomes that have arisen from the decisions you have made. Reflecting on your practice will help you understand the direction you are headed (Mendez, 2021). As you continue to enhance this leadership quality, consider the following questions to help jump start and guide your reflective practice:

- How was my day today?
- How was the day for my teachers and our young learners/scholars?
- What actions did I take to benefit students, teachers, and our overall school community?
- What was challenging today?
- Why was the situation challenging?
- What steps did I take to alleviate the challenge?
- How did my actions impact my team?
- How did I demonstrate kindness today?
- Was I visibly present today?
- Did I give myself time to tune into my building's pulse? What stood out?
- How will I utilize today's reflection to help guide tomorrow's decisions?

It is important to maintain an open mind when focused on enhancing your reflective leadership style. It is not about arriving at all the right answers. Rather, the reflective process is aimed at gaining perspective on your actions, understanding outcomes, and learning from past mistakes to enhance your leadership skills and strengthen relationships with critical stakeholders.

One of our favorite quotes is "It is not about being the best. It is about being better than you were yesterday." As an educational leader, you will often hear experts in the field discussing best practices. Of course, it is important to know what the research suggests about our field and how to apply those understandings to daily practice. At the same time, it is crucial to reflect on how things are currently working (or not) and what you can do to design solutions that ultimately impact the growth and development of your students.

Turning "Epic Fails" into Amazing Innovations

Through the process of reflective leadership, you will gain an understanding of your mistakes and will use your newfound knowledge to help guide your future successes. To demonstrate that not all failures or mistakes result in catastrophe, we chose to highlight and discuss a few "epic fails" made by new leaders as they transition into their leadership role. We hope these epic fails allow you to see the positive side of failure.

Epic Fail 1: Not Meeting Deadlines

Lack of time management: Often, many leaders claim that there are not enough hours in the day to accomplish the tasks necessary to meet leadership demands. This results in the creation of difficult situations that end up leaving leaders feeling frustrated and stressed out. New leaders need to develop an awareness of time and how to use it productively. If this speaks to you, do not stress! The key is to learn to prioritize your work-related activities so that you can quickly solve or complete high priority tasks first. One helpful idea that can support your time management skills is the creation of a "To Do" list. Prior to ending your workday, think about what issues need to be addressed and tasks need to be completed. Upon your arrival the next day, tackle your list by order of priority. Upon your arrival to work the next day, you will already have an action plan ready to go! Checking off items on your "To Do" list will help you feel good about getting the work done.

Leadership tip: There are many research-based organizational tools that you can use to keep on top of your tasks at-hand. While post-its are helpful for jotting down information, they can quickly build up and leave folks feeling frustrated. This overwhelming feeling can lead many to choose to accomplish none of the tasks rather than to prioritize, and at least start, some of the tasks. Invest in an organizational management tool that works for you. Also, brain-storm solutions with your colleagues. Appendix A includes a list of useful tools for organization and communication. We suggest giving each a try until you find the tool that is just right for you.

Epic Fail 2: Taking on Too Much to Handle

Lack of delegating tasks: New leaders make the mistake of thinking they must do "all the things" themselves. Effective leaders understand that they cannot do it all alone. We have seen many new leaders burn out because they lack the leadership ability to delegate. Delegating is an art. It requires you to identify members of your team that can help you get the work done. Delegating tasks to other qualified members of your team will free up time for you to take care of other pertinent actions. In the end, you will accomplish more tasks when delegating and sharing the workload. However, be mindful of how you approach the delegation of tasks. Simply passing your work along for others to do while you sit back and relax is not an effective leadership trait. Your action may cause resentment and burn out among your team. Refer back to Chapter 7 for a discussion on leadership styles.

Leadership tip: Be aware of what tasks could and should be delegated and what tasks should not. If a task involves sensitive information about the students you serve or the teachers you supervise, be sure to follow regulations around how that data and information are shared. There are times when you may want to move around and play with the data in a format that is more manual, but time consuming. While more streamlined data entry and reporting are helpful, having a physical and tangible look at the information can lead to different types of solutions and insights. Recognize that you may not be able to do all of the tasks on your own. Elicit the help of your leadership team in deciphering and analyzing data.

Epic Fail 3: Falling Victim to Status Quo Mentality

Victim of complacency: When embarking on your first leadership role, you know it is not easy to effect change. You also know that change takes time. However, it is important for you to understand that complacency does not yield innovation. We work in environments where the only constant is change. A failure to challenge complacency generates leaders who are fearful of new ideas, thinking, and perspectives. Be a changemaker by critically looking at your school, by analyzing all relevant school data, and by beginning to take measures to challenge the status quo mentality. Your role is to create learning environments that prepare students for the future. To accomplish this task, you must break away from being a victim of complacent thinking. Consider the following example: You are seeking medical advice and have two doctors to choose from. The first offers a traditional explanation and solely relies on "We've always done it this way." The second offers an explanation that recognizes how practices around solutions to your medical concern have evolved. Who would you trust in helping you achieve your goals?

Epic Fail 4: Being Trapped by Imposter Syndrome

Victim of imposter syndrome: Imposter syndrome is a real phenomenon that causes individuals to feel like they are not as competent as others around them. It is a continuous pattern of self-doubt in one's potential. These feelings can mentally impede a leader's abilities to fully express themselves in front of others, ask questions, or engage in discussion. The trick to fighting imposter syndrome is to avoid comparing yourself to others. You must acknowledge that you do not know everything and that it is okay to take the time to research, learn, and prepare. Build confidence by trying. Learn from the mistakes you make. Believe that every day is a new day to try again. Remember that you should never compare your first chapter to someone else's Chapter 20. In Chapter 10 we engage in discussions around lifelong learning. Embracing a lifelong learner mindset will help eradicate imposter syndrome.

Being in a position of leadership is both difficult and demanding. Each day brings a new challenge, and often we are left feeling like complete and total failures. Do not let these epic fails hold you down. Take a deep breath and remember that mistakes are proof that you are trying. In the following section, we share with you strategies that can help you mitigate and handle stress and stressful situations.

Self-Care for Early Childhood Leaders

We previously mentioned that early childhood and primary school leaders are tasked with making decisions that impact students, teachers, and staff on a daily basis. Some decisions may not be popular with the masses. This can cause a great deal of stress and pressure on the lives of school leaders. Such stressors can lead to health problems, lack of sleep, and untimely burn-out. To prevent such burn-out, it is imperative that early childhood and primary school leaders practice self-care. The act of self-care is defined as one's ability to act toward preserving or improving one's personal health. There is no right or wrong way to practice self-care. Self-care is based on what an individual person finds joy in doing. The following includes four different self-care focus areas along with questions to consider when thinking about implementing a self-care routine that will enhance your daily life as an educational leader.

> **Physical self-care:** Maintaining a consistent exercise routine can help support your immune system allowing you to feel good. Focus on your physical well-being by creating time and opportunity to exercise. An early morning exercise routine can help energize your body and lead to a successful start to your day. Eating healthy will help generate the energy needed to get you through the day. Planning and preparing your daily meals is key. Have a nice mix of greens,

fruits, and protein to fuel your body. Ensure you pack healthy snack options, too. As leaders we all know that time literally flies when things come up and the day is hectic; however, do ensure that you are taking the time to eat your breakfast, lunch, and snacks throughout the day. Skipping your meals or snacks can negatively impact your physical health. Sleep is an important component to maintaining a healthy body. Most adults need anywhere between seven to nine hours of sleep to feel their best. Make sure you are providing your body with the time it needs to recover from the stressors of the day. Together, these self-care routines will help you feel good, be well rested, and allow you to think clearly when making decisions. When thinking about your physical health, consider the following questions:

Questions to Consider

On most days, do I lack energy?
Am I allocating time for exercise?
Am I getting enough sleep?
Am I getting enough rest?
Am I eating healthy foods?
How many meals did I have today?
How many ounces of water did I drink?

Social self-care: Human beings are social beings. Therefore, it is important for school leaders to maintain positive relationships outside of the work environment with their friends and family. Spending time with friends and family discussing life events, enjoying each other's company, and talking about other things that are not work-related helps leaders maintain a healthy work–life balance. We have heard school leaders share their frustrations on the amount of work they do and how work limits their time and ability to get together with friends and family. We challenge you to find ways to reignite and strengthen your social relationships. While we all love our jobs, and understand the importance of the work we do, taking time to do other things will help relieve work-related stress giving way for joy, happiness, and fulfillment. Value your personal time! It is easy to find yourself answering emails on a Saturday afternoon because you obviously care about the work you do and know that it matters to your teams, teachers, staff members, and students. However, time taken away from family and friends impedes your own personal well-being. This can lead toward feelings of resentment, frustration, and burn-out. Prioritize your family and their needs. Being present in your family's lives will help your mental health and will support an effective work–life balance. When practicing social self-care reflect upon the following:

Questions to Consider

Am I allocating quality time for family and friends?
Do I look forward to the weekend?
Do I partake in a hobby or activity that brings me joy?
Am I spending enough time with my family?
How much work do I take home on the weekends?
How frequently do I check work emails while at home?

Professional self-care: As a leader, you want to make yourself available to your students, teachers, staff members, parents, colleagues, and all the other constituents that have a stake in the success of your school. However, the reality is that there is only ONE of you to go around! Do not make the mistake of spreading yourself so thin that you unintentionally create unnecessary stress. Learn to set boundaries for yourself. Leverage your clerks' ability to organize and schedule your meetings. Share calendars with your administrative team so everyone is aware of your availability. Embed time for checking and responding to emails, making and returning phone calls, and do not forget the importance of scheduling time for your informal and formal walkthroughs. In Chapter 2 we discussed the importance of creating a schedule for visiting classrooms. This is a crucial component of your day. Limit work-related stress through shared leadership and collaboration with your teams. Refer to Chapter 7 to learn more about leadership styles that may help improve your ability to manage your professional responsibilities and improve your team's overall effectiveness. Professional self-care also calls for your ability to enhance your leadership skills through professional development and new learning opportunities. Consider joining a professional organization and engaging in interest-based professional development. This can help you see problems differently, gather new ideas, and put learning into practice. Learning new things can enhance your leadership effectiveness and help reduce work-related stress. When practicing professional self-care, reflect upon the following:

Questions to Consider

How much time do I devote to work issues after hours?
Do I have established boundaries?
How is my relationship with colleagues?
Is stress at work affecting my family life and routines?
Do I have a grasp on work–life balance?
Am I a member of a professional support group?
How frequently do I engage in opportunities to learn new
   skills and enhance my leadership abilities?

Emotional self-care: We opened this chapter with the mantra, "mistakes are proof that I am trying." We want you to internalize this and begin to see mistakes as mere opportunities for growth. Therefore, when you make a mistake, do not dwell on it. Instead, be kind and forgiving to yourself. Reflect, refocus, and try again. We also want you to understand and acknowledge the relationship between emotions, feelings, and work performance. If you are feeling down, defeated, stressed, or overworked your work performance will be negatively impacted. You will not be your best self, and your output may diminish. Additionally, your subconscious may begin to form negative emotions that will impact your perspective on work, career choice, and sometimes even life. There are many ways that can help you sort out, acknowledge, and practice emotional self-care. Among the popular and effective ones are journaling and meditation. Through journaling, you can spend time writing about your feelings and emotions. The act itself allows you to gain a deeper understanding of the issue you are dealing with. The process will help shed light on possible solutions to problems and elicit feelings of confidence and self-awareness. Meditation helps you become in tune with your mind and body. This practice helps to release stress, improves feelings of well-being, and supports mental health. When practicing emotional self-care, reflect on the following:

Questions to Consider

Am I practicing care and kindness with myself?
Am I practicing positive self-talk?
Can I express or share my feelings?
How much time do I devote to meditating?
What are the things that have caused me emotional stress?
How do I regulate my feelings and emotions?

In order to be a successful leader, you must take self-care seriously. To serve others, you must be the best YOU you can be. Practicing self-care is not selfish. It is a way to prioritize your mental and physical health. This can only be achieved when self-care is made a priority. We have described four essential areas for self-care: Physical, emotional, professional, and social self-care. When analyzing your self-care status, consider reflecting on the questions included under each self-care category as a starting point to help guide practice. Ensure that you acknowledge areas of strength while identifying areas that are in need of improvement. The next section of this chapter will help you begin to think about developing your self-care plan.

Creating an Action Plan That Works for You

In Chapter 6, we spoke about tools that support the work you do as leaders. One suggestion we mentioned was the use of calendars and planners to facilitate your schedules and day to day activities. Being intentional about planning will help keep you on track with your classroom visits and student interactions and help guide your visibility. Just as you are intentional about planning and scheduling your daily classroom visits and meetings, etc., you must be intentional about planning and scheduling your self-care routines. Given the importance of your personal social, emotional, and mental health, your ability to focus and institute a self-care practice is not an option. It is essential to your overall health and effectiveness. By being intentional about your self-care, you will be successful in creating not just a self-care plan but a self-care ritual.

To lead others, you must make sure you are the best possible version of you. This includes feeling your best so that you maximize your ability to think critically and make good decisions in the interest of your students, teachers, and staff. A self-care action plan will help you stick to your goals and help you prioritize your personal needs. When creating your self-care action plan, find a format that is conducive to your lifestyle and your needs. Some people prefer to create a list of things that bring them joy and refer to the list when they know that they need time to recharge. Others like to use their planners and embed self-care time into their weekly or monthly spreads. We suggest you use a mix of both. Below we include a few ideas to help you create your own self-care plan.

Make the list: Your self-care list should include ideas that will support opportunities for both quick pick me ups or longer recharge sessions. Your list can be created in several different formats. You can choose to have a simple composition notebook to jot down the list of things you like to do and refer to them when you are ready to do them. You can use a digital word processor to keep track of your list. Whatever you decide, your list should be easy to follow, maintain, and retrieve. Do not overthink it! If it is conducive to your well-being, add it to the list. Examples of quick pick me ups may include:

- Brunch with friends
- Trip to the hair salon
- A work out session

- A personal massage
- Manicure and pedicure time
- Relaxation time in the sauna
- Trip to the bookstore
- Coffee or movie date
- Listening to your favorite music tunes
- Watching a favorite television show, etc.

There really are endless possibilities for quick pick me ups because these are based on you, your needs, and whatever brings you joy. It is important to maintain this list so that you are able to refer to it, select from, and enjoy the things that make you happy.

In addition to quick pick me ups, self-care may also include opportunities for longer recharge sessions. These are necessary when you need more time to reflect and recover from stress and its impact on your well-being. Use long-term planning to schedule these recharge sessions. For example, you may want to plan a weekend getaway when schools are observing a four-day weekend. Or, you may plan a spa and meditation retreat while school is on winter or spring break. Use your school calendars to look for opportunities to take a much-needed self-care retreat. During these times, it is important to focus on YOU. If you must check your email, allow yourself an hour per day. If it cannot be done in that hour, do what you can and continue the next day. The point is that you must maximize your break from work. Taking a break is not the same as working from home! Allowing an hour per day will enable you to keep up to date with your work responsibilities while benefiting from taking the time to focus on yourself. Sometimes, the act of just being in your own space, without disturbances, or timelines, can give you the necessary jolt you need to recharge, refocus, and be reenergized. Self-care is not selfish; it is our responsibility to maintain healthy bodies and minds.

Being intentional: To maintain your commitment to self-care routines, be intentional about including them in your weekly and long-term plans. We suggest that you actively review your self-care lists and select one or two ideas to add to your weekly plans. For example, try including a coffee date with a friend, a yoga class, a trip to the barber shop, or the nail salon. When you plan ahead, you are more likely to follow through with your plans. Therefore, plan for self-care opportunities just as you plan your weekly observations and classroom visits. Sticking to your plans will help develop your self-care habits and eventually transform some of them into self-care rituals that are an intentional and indispensable component in ensuring that you are socially, emotionally, and mentally healthy. Make the commitment to prioritize yourself and your well-being. Remember, there is only one YOU!

Leadership tip: Create a self-care vision board. Vision boards are visual representations of your goals and aspirations. They typically include pictures, words, and phrases that are meaningful to you. They serve as positive visual affirmations that can help us manifest our goals. Vision boards help you focus on your goals and maintain positive self-talk. By creating your self-care vision board, you can begin to manifest and prioritize all the things that bring you joy. We suggest creating quarterly self-care vision boards. This will allow you to try new things, reach short-term goals, and remain focused and committed to practicing and developing your self-care routines.

Eye on equity: We cannot help but consider and mention the stress caused by COVID-19 upon our schools, teachers, staff, students, families, communities, and school leadership teams. We hope that you also acknowledge that although self-care is essential to our overall well-being, it is a notion that may be out of grasp for some of our students and their families. In Chapter 2 we discussed the importance of cultivating caring and responsive learning environments. With this in mind, we challenge you to embed opportunities to practice self-care into your schools. Consider guided meditation via the web-based application Calm to teach students the importance of tuning into their minds and bodies. Perhaps your parents and caregivers would enjoy a late afternoon snack and meditation session with their children. Be creative in thinking about ways to bring self-care to your school. If it helps you as a leader, imagine how it can help your students and their families.

Critical Friends

Oftentimes, leadership can be a lonesome journey. Your role implies power. This perception of power could potentially cause fear and can leave you being surrounded by people who will never tell you the truth. In fact, you may find yourself surrounded by people who will consistently tell you what you want to hear. It is not that they want to be dishonest; rather, they may be deterred from expressing themselves because you are in a position of power. That, however, is no way to lead. You need to listen to different perspectives, and you need people to challenge your thinking. A critical friend is someone who can help you look at situations through a different lens or point of view. This individual will listen to your arguments, situations, struggles, and concerns with the understanding that they will provide you with unbiased feedback (Mendez, 2021). The beauty of critical friendships is the fact that they WILL tell you how it is! They will not sugar coat anything. If something does not appear to be right, they will question it. Critical friends are essential to your professional growth and development.

Final Thoughts

When mistakes happen, opportunities for reflection arise, and learning occurs. Do not let the fear of failure or making mistakes prevent you from trying new things. Do not let the fear of failure prevent you from implementing new ideas. Do not let the fear of failure prevent you from growing. Adopt a reflective leadership style that enables you to analyze, deconstruct, learn from, and ultimately bounce back stronger from any epic failure. Leverage the minds of your administrative team. Engage in the sharing of ideas, the breaking down of tasks, and the benefit of collaborating and working to achieve a common goal. Acknowledge that although you are the leader in charge, you must give attention to your emotional, social, physical, and mental needs. Be intentional about practicing self-care. Create a list of things that help you destress and that bring you joy. Practice those things without limitations. Be kind to yourself and stick to your self-care action plan. Lastly, consider establishing a critical friend relationship at work. Such will help you reflect on your decisions based on their unbiased feedback.

Chapter 9: Reflection Questions

- What causes stress in my life?
- How do I deal with stress?
- How am I prioritizing myself and my needs?
- What brings me joy?
- Do I allow myself to be and live in the moment?

Chapter 9: Failing Forward as an Early Childhood Changemaker

Leadership Action Spotlight

Identify three takeaways from Chapter 9.

_____

_____

_____

Write down two ideas that you would like to implement in your current role.

OR for aspiring leaders

Write down two ideas that you would consider implementing in the future.

_____

_____

_____

Identify one lingering question or area you would like to explore further.

_____

_____

_____

Personal reflection, thoughts, comments, concerns, ideas:

_____

_____

_____

_____

_____

From "Better" to "Best"

10

Committing to Lifelong Learning

Positive Affirmation: I Welcome Change and Grow from Experiences

Almost everything that occurs in our society has an impact on education. Hence, educational leaders must be ready to embrace change and cultivate learning environments that are responsive to the needs of students, parents, teachers, and staff. However, this is no easy feat as many individuals view change as a threat that may result in failure. Equating change with failure is among the many reasons why some people are fearful of change. Fear of failure can prevent school leaders from exploring new opportunities for their schools. In contrast, leaders should view the challenges created by change as new experiences and opportunities to enhance their professional growth.

****

Beyond the Cliche: What Is Lifelong Learning?

The Greek philosopher, Heraclitus, once said "change is the only constant in life." With time, we have grown accustomed to linking change with struggle. Consequently, many individuals fear change and inadvertently limit their learning and growth. It is easy to fall victim to the minutiae of routines and mindsets that do not look beyond the traditional. However, our world is driven by innovation. Think of how amid the COVID-19 pandemic, our education system was able to transform brick-and-mortar schooling into virtual classrooms. This tremendous feat was only made possible because of technological advancements. Schools driven by leaders who embraced

DOI: 10.4324/9781003219767-13

these changes made modifications to how they communicated and engaged with students, parents, teachers, and staff. These leaders adapted to the change and continued to foster positive learning environments driven by the needs of their students. If we learned one thing from the resulting chaos of the pandemic, it was the fact that change can spring upon us at any given time. As leaders, we must make the choice to develop a learning mindset focused on growth.

The term "lifelong learner" has obtained a great deal of notoriety in the last few years. In fact, it has become a popular social media hashtag. But what exactly constitutes a lifelong learner? What are some characteristics of lifelong learning? Why is lifelong learning an important leadership skill? The answers to these questions revolve around growth, development, and embracing a learning mindset. Let's take some time to dig deeper into these questions.

What Constitutes a Lifelong Learner?

Lifelong learning is defined as a process through which individuals obtain, comprehend, and manipulate the knowledge they have acquired through learning and personal experiences. Lifelong learning is about growth. Individuals with aspirations to succeed often engage in learning activities beyond traditional schooling and degree seeking opportunities. They pursue opportunities to advance and expand their skill sets. These learners aspire to achieve either professional or personal fulfillment. Lifelong learners are people who understand the notion that things, people, places, and ideas are constantly evolving.

What Are Some Characteristics of Lifelong Learners?

Lifelong learners are driven by intrinsic motivation. They possess the drive and discipline to find and engage in either independent learning or self-directed studies. They are readers, thinkers, and innovators who view change as opportunities. They are solution seekers with a strong sense of who they are, how they learn, and what motivates them to achieve.

Why Is Lifelong Learning an Important Leadership Skill?

Leaders with foresight on change coupled with the desire to continuously learn can adapt to unexpected situations. They are committed to innovation and the disruption of the status quo mentality. These leaders understand the need to search for answers, to seek guidance when problems arise, and to prepare for potential issues that may cause harm to their institutions. They can listen to different perspectives and leverage ideas that are best suited for their schools. Lifelong learning keeps the mind open to new possibilities.

A learning mindset will prepare you to face the unknown. Leaders who embrace a learning mindset are capable of listening to and learning from others. They welcome collaborative partnerships that can help increase teacher and staff efficacy resulting in increased student achievement.

Leadership tip: Lifelong learning is a commitment to continuous growth and development. To keep up to date with the fast-changing world of education, register for professional organizations such as the International Literacy Association (ILA) or the Association for Supervision and Curriculum Development (ASCD). These organizations distribute newsletters, quarterly magazines, books, etc., featuring articles on different topics such as educational leadership, technology, curriculum, and assessments. Our Favorite Resources feature a list of our top professional organizations for you to peruse.

Eye on equity: It is important that you become a member of organizations that offer diversity in voice. Ensure that your learning engagements are conducive to the needs of those you serve. Focus on increasing your knowledge and awareness about inequities impacting your students' abilities to get a fair and equity driven education. Aspire to be informed about strategies that help reduce bias and deficit mindsets. Share new ideas and promote learning during faculty meetings, and share out resources with your teams. Put learning into action, and help promote cultures driven by inclusivity and equity.

The Problem with "We've Always Done Things This Way"

In education, we use the term status quo as a reference to the forces that impact learning, teaching, and leading in schools. These forces are inclusive of but not limited to instructional policies, curriculum practices, and the structures that impact learning. Schools led by visionary lifelong learners have a grasp on their stakeholders' needs in relation to the demands of the world we live in. These leaders challenge the status quo to infuse learning mindsets capable of adapting to change and acquiring growth. When considering education, development, and learning we must consider the idea of change. B.F. Skinner (Schunk, 2020) defined learning as a response to, or a change in behavior resulting from reinforcement. Skinner's theory suggests that learning is a function of change.

When leaders refuse the idea of change, they are affirming the "we've always done things this way" mindset. This type of thinking hinders you and your school's ability to grow, develop, and achieve success in a world that is constantly undergoing change. Institutions driven by status quo mentalities are doing their students a disservice. Take for instance social media. While it has its drawbacks, social media has become a means through which parents have voiced concerns, connected with other parents, or gone on tirades about what schools are doing or not doing to help students. Leaders who were not afraid of social media took to the different platforms to share all the wonderful happenings, engagement opportunities, and information relevant to their respective school. With the help of social media, school leaders challenged the status quo and were able to utilize the different platforms to share their school's narrative. In doing so, they disrupted the flow of inaccurate information being shared by others.

Disrupting the status quo requires a degree of risk taking. Many leaders experience fear when faced with risks. The most prevalent fear is that of failing. After all, failure is the opposite of success and how can we develop the courage to disrupt the status quo when faced with the possibility of failure? Leaders who embrace a learning mindset see failure as opportunities. In Chapter 9 we presented you with the idea that failure stimulates reflection. It provides leaders with opportunities to think about the choices they made and the outcomes of those choices. The reflection process helps shed light on what could have been done or approached differently. This process creates space necessary for growth.

Leadership tip: There will be times during your educational career where you will have to challenge the status quo to ensure that students have equitable early childhood learning experiences. Consider the following example: Students in your school are engaged in a reading and writing workshop model, but many striving readers are struggling to master their reading foundational skills. While the structure of the school day may prohibit changes, you suggest piloting a new intervention program and flexibly adapting the schedule to make services available for those students.

While these changes will not be easy, or occur overnight for that matter, they help to ensure that students are set up for success as early readers. Considering this scenario, can you think of other examples that exist in your school community?

Eye on equity: Disrupting the status quo or advocating for change can sometimes be interpreted as characteristics of overly passionate or troublesome leaders. If you have ever experienced such labels, do not feel ashamed, embarrassed, or defeated. Know that you are often speaking and advocating for the needs of marginalized youth who count on you to continue to advocate for their needs. Keep doing the work necessary to challenge traditions that are no longer serving our children.

Choose Your Path: Committing to Learning and Excellence

We previously suggested obtaining memberships in professional organizations as a way to jumpstart a lifelong learning mindset. We would now like to explore five additional ways through which you can embrace a lifelong learning mindset to enhance your professional growth and development as leaders.

Traditional Certification Courses

While you may not have the time, energy, or even resources to invest in an additional major or graduate program of study, there are traditional certification routes that can help you expand your practice. We lean on our own personal experiences as early childhood leaders to share how we continue to grow and develop as we stay committed to excellence for our young scholars. In the communities we serve, many students are English learners. This population continues to grow and comes with its own unique needs and challenges. By engaging in sheltered instruction and Sheltered Instruction Observation Protocol (SIOP) courses, we have learned new ways to advocate for English learners, while enhancing our daily learning objectives to include engaging opportunities for students to "play" with language. We take advantage of course offerings that even lead to English as a Second Language (ESL) certification in as little as two college semesters. These opportunities help to grow and enhance your repertoire as an educational leader. Given the increased use of technology, many colleges and universities offer traditional certification, masters, specialists, and doctoral coursework online. Because they can be done in the comfort of your own home, online programs are increasing in popularity among working professionals.

Nontraditional Certification Courses

Another way to enhance your leadership skills is through nontraditional certification courses. Many school leaders have pursued certifications that have been beneficial to their instructional positions. For example, one popular certification program is the Mindful Teacher Certification program offered through Mindful Schools. This certification program provides teachers and school leaders with strategies to support the social and emotional well-being of students with the aid of trauma-sensitive practices. This is just one example of a nontraditional certification course that can serve to enhance your leadership skills. There are others such as *Inquiry Driven Leadership* provided through the MIT Sloan School of Management, or the *Leadership and Management* certification program offered through the Harvard Business School Online.

Professional Development Sessions

Attending professional development sessions is one way to continue to develop your leadership skills. Many organizations set up leadership retreats or summits that focus on different topics around leadership, curriculum and instructions, culturally responsive practices, etc. The topics are truly endless. If you seek opportunities for professional development, you will find that you will encounter different perspectives which will help you improve your own leadership skills. As we write this text, many organizations are offering virtual options for professional development, too. Some of our favorite professional development opportunities include but are not limited to:

- VIBE-PD, organized by Robert Jackson, @RJMotivates
- ASCD Annual Conferences and Leadership Summit, organized by the Association for Supervision and Curriculum Development, @ASCD
- NJPSA/FEA/NJASCD Annual Conferences, organized by New Jersey Principals and Supervisors Association, @NJPSA
- NBOE Women's Leadership Conference, organized by Newark Board of Education Deputy Superintendent Nicole T. Johnson

Leadership tip: Connect with local and state professional organizations in order to stay informed about professional development and professional learning opportunities that are part of your calendar year. At the same time, many national organizations offer webinars and on-demand digital learning events that you can access at your own leisure. When events may pique the interest of other leaders in your building, be sure to share the offerings with your team and consider hosting a "watch event." The sharing of key ideas and insights after participating in professional development conferences helps to cultivate a community of learners. Keep the fire going by challenging your teams to implement strategies and share out the outcomes.

Reading and Professional Book Studies

Reading is a must for lifelong learners. There are books written for relatively all areas of instructional leadership, teaching, learning, and development. If there is an area or skill set you would like to develop in, head to your local bookstore and browse through the titles. The wonderful thing about reading is that you can do it alone yet engage in group discussions about the insights gained from reading. Professional book studies allow for open discussions in which participants share their understandings, wonderings, and perspectives on a text. Often, strategies obtained from reading a text are deployed in classrooms or leadership meetings. Participants reflect on the strategy implementation and share those reflections with the members of the book club. This interchanging of ideas, thought-provoking questions, and the results of putting theories into practice facilitates the collective growth and development of the club's members. Web-based communication applications such as Zoom, Webex, and Google Hangouts have increased the use of professional book studies in education.

Professional Learning Network

A professional learning network (PLN) consists of a group of individuals who are committed to lifelong learning. They engage in informal discussions about different topics, share perspectives on situations, and help one another come up with practical solutions to problems. PLN meetings can occur in person such as the informal CoffeeEDU groups that frequently meet on the weekends in local coffee shops. Most meetings and discussions occur through virtual and digital platforms such as Twitter, Facebook, and Voxer. Whether you are new to the profession or are a veteran leader, joining a PLN can be a great way to continue to learn and grow.

As you embark on your leadership journey, be sure to embrace and develop a lifelong learning mindset. Looking for opportunities to engage in learning whether through traditional or nontraditional means will allow you to keep abreast of changes that impact education. Your participation will also help to keep you motivated and focused on improving student outcomes.

Eye on equity: When selecting areas of interest and development needs, consider the role you play in supporting and advocating for your students, teachers, and staff. Look for development opportunities that provide strategies and discussions around building positive relationships, motivating and engaging stakeholders, strengthening the home and school connection, and the fostering of inclusive practices. While this is not an exhaustive list by any means, engaging in learning opportunities that foster growth and development is the goal of lifelong learning.

Final Thoughts

Change can awaken the fear of failure in instructional leaders. Leaders that give in to this fear neglect the possibility that change can also bring about positive outcomes. Failure is a reality that should not deter leaders from trying something new. When failure occurs, it is essential to look at the situation, reflect on the outcome, and make adjustments that will ensure future success. To achieve this, leaders must embrace a lifelong learning mindset. There are several ways leaders can adopt a lifelong learning mindset. Through nontraditional certification courses, participating in professional development, and engaging in reading and professional book studies, as well as in joining professional learning networks, instructional leaders can adopt a learning mindset that will help them perceive change as opportunities for growth.

Our Favorite Chapter Resource Links

- International Literacy Association (ILA): http://www.reading.org
- Association for Supervision and Curriculum Development (ASCD): https://www.ascd.org
- National Association for the Education of Young Children (NAEYC): : https://www.naeyc.org
- Childhood Education International (CE International): https://ceinternational1892.org
- International Society for Technology Education (ISTE): https://www.iste.org
- National Education Association (NEA): https://www.nea.org/about-nea

---

Chapter 10: Reflection Questions

- What are my perspectives on change?
- How am I enhancing my leadership skills?
- Which professional organizations do I belong to?
- How can I engage in lifelong learning?
- Am I a part of a professional learning network?

Chapter 10: From "Better" to "Best": Committing to Lifelong Learning

Leadership Action Spotlight

Identify three takeaways from Chapter 10.

_____
_____
_____

Write down two ideas that you would like to implement in your current role.

OR for aspiring leaders

Write down two ideas that you would consider implementing in the future.

_____
_____
_____

Identify one lingering question or area you would like to explore further.

_____

_____

_____

Personal reflection, thoughts, comments, concerns, ideas:

_____

_____

_____

_____

_____

Concluding Thoughts

This book was written and intended to help guide and support educators transitioning into the role of early childhood leadership. We began by identifying the importance of having a commitment to understanding early childhood, primary school settings, and the conditions needed for young learners to blossom and grow in school. We identified our overarching purpose or "why" in stating our first mantra, the work that we do really matters. These positive affirmations continued throughout the chapters to help establish a framework driven by the role leaders play in supporting young learners.

Throughout the remainder of the text, we advocated for the importance of taking joy in the process. We suggested the adoption of lifelong learning and equity driven mindsets. As leaders in education, you must be committed to finding a way to consistently engage with early childhood research, theories, and best practices. Let's revisit our affirmations and how they come together and guide your journey as an emerging early childhood leader.

Part I: A Glimpse into the World of Early Childhood

Chapter 1: *The work I do really matters.*

Chapter 2: *I can positively impact students' lives.*

Chapter 3: *I feel joy when students receive the support they need.*

Part II: Understanding Teaching, Learning, Student Engagement, and Recognition in Early Childhood Settings

Chapter 4: *I can ignite a love for learning.*

Chapter 5: *I can design a learning agenda that builds students' background knowledge and passion for critical thinking.*

DOI: 10.4324/9781003219767-14

Chapter 6: *I feel accomplished when students are learning.*

Part III: Leading in Early Childhood Settings

Chapter 7: *I know my purpose.*

Chapter 8: *I am intentional about cultivating an inclusive culture.*

Chapter 9: *Mistakes are proof that I am trying.*

Chapter 10: *I welcome change and grow from experiences.*

First and foremost, we believe in your discovery as an emerging leader and have faith that you are now equipped to stop and check the pulse of how you feel as an early childhood leader. Given the affirmations above, where are your strengths? What are you going to prioritize and work on as a short-term goal? What are your long-term goals? To solidify a commitment to this work, we strongly suggest keeping a journal—a physical reminder to put out in the universe that this work is ongoing and just the beginning of how your advocacy for young learners will take shape. As you revisit each of the earlier chapters, use the prompts at the end to build out your goals. This is an opportunity for you to become more specific and determine the following:

- What Tier 1 (immediate) goals will help you ASAP in the early childhood setting?

- What Tier 2 (long-term) goals will help you successfully navigate in the direction you are heading?

Early childhood leaders need to reflect on these resources, leadership action possibilities, and reflection prompts as a launching pad for the work that lies ahead.

How can this work be done?

- Document your goals, and surround yourself with accountability partners and a network of early childhood leaders.

- Commit to joining professional organizations and voluminous reading. Extended opportunities for reading about your field and early childhood settings will undoubtedly spark new ideas and insights while strengthening your background knowledge.

This book was designed to get you started in your journey as an early childhood leader. Of course, we strongly believe that your self-direction as an adult learner will allow you to think about your own needs, consider different strategies for being successful, and evaluate how things go. Even as we look back on our years of combined experience in early childhood settings, we are often amazed at how the field continues to move forward with new insights, discoveries, and innovations that impact child development. Be proud of your role in this incredibly joyous work, know that you are indeed making a difference and sowing the seeds for a more rich and robust future, and lead with conviction.

With gratitude,

—Elaine and Ken

End of Chapter Reflection Questions

Part I: A Glimpse into the World of Early Childhood

Chapter 1: Understanding Early Childhood and Primary School Settings

- What implications do learning theories have for early childhood learners?
- How am I helping my teams enhance learning and developing opportunities for students?
- What systems of student support do I have in place?
- How do I know that the needs of my students are considered by my staff?

Chapter 2: Cultivating a Caring and Responsive Learning Environment

- How will you make your mark in your school?
- How will you show your students that you care?
- How will you demonstrate care to teachers and staff?
- What strategies will help you develop a caring and responsive learning environment?

Chapter 3: Promoting Students' Social, Emotional, and Academic Growth

- What systems are in place to help my teachers and grade level teams meet the needs of students?
- Are there strategies in place to support the social and emotional development of all?
- How are my grade level teams addressing behavior concerns?
- How am I promoting an inclusive learning environment?

Part II: Understanding Teaching, Learning, Student Engagement, and Recognition in Early Childhood Settings

Chapter 4: Standing Out as a "Lit" Early Childhood Leader

- Are my teachers' literacy schedules conducive to the needs of the students?
- Are teachers conducting small group instruction? If so, how often?
- Are the classrooms print rich and inclusive of students' developmental needs?
- How am I promoting literacy practices in school?
- How am I engaging families and advocating for an ongoing partnership?

Chapter 5: Learning and Leading Strategies to Support Content Area Instruction

- When you look back on your preparation as a teacher or educational leader, what subject areas are a strength in your toolkit? What areas would you like to learn more about?
- What opportunities exist in your school year for curriculum development teams to meet and explore issues raised in this chapter, among others that are presented in your individual school community?

- Are there any gaps that exist in your educational programming?
- How else might you ensure that your budding scholars are receiving a strong foundation for future college and career success?
- Is an emphasis on social and emotional learning (SEL) evident throughout curricular programs?
- What other content is needed for your young learners?

Chapter 6: Spotting and Recognizing Student Engagement and Intentional Learning

- How am I managing my time efficiently?
- Are my students reflected in my school's curriculum?
- What am I doing to support my teachers to do the work that needs to be done?
- How am I communicating with parents, caretakers, and community partners?
- How frequently am I engaged with students?
- Am I familiar with my district's policies around the topics highlighted in this chapter?

Part III: Leading in Early Childhood Settings

Chapter 7: Identifying Your Leadership Style

- What type of relationship do I want to have with my leadership team?
- How will I distribute the workload?
- Will I be guided by individual strengths or interests?
- How will I involve my team in the decision-making process?
- Are first languages and bilingual learners celebrated for their cultural assets?
- How will I hold others accountable?
- How will I enable opportunities for teacher leadership? Sharing ideas?

Chapter 8: Refining Our Leadership Approach through Culturally Responsive Practices

- Based on the chapter, consider how well you know your students.
- Do you invite and involve families in inclusive ways?
- How are students' identities respected, cultivated, and developed across the curriculum?
- Are first languages and bilingual learners celebrated for their cultural assets?
- Are spaces designed to include conversations with teachers around culturally responsive teaching as they enhance their practice?

Chapter 9: Failing Forward as an Early Childhood Changemaker

- What causes stress in my life?
- How do I deal with stress?
- How am I prioritizing myself and my needs?
- What brings me joy?
- Do I allow myself to be and live in the moment?

Chapter 10: From "Better" to "Best": Committing to Lifelong Learning

- What are my perspectives on change?
- How am I enhancing my leadership skills?
- Which professional organizations do I belong to?
- How can I engage in lifelong learning?
- Am I a part of a professional learning network?

Appendix

List of Tools for Organization and Communication

Organization Tools

- Google Suite
  - Google Drive
  - Google Forms
  - Google Sheets
  - Google Keep
  - Google Calendar
- Outlook
- Calendly
- Dropbox
- Evernote

Communication Tools:

- Slack
- Remind
- Voxer
- Smore
- Flipboard
- WebEx
- Zoom

- Google Hangouts
- Flipgrid
- Instagram
- Facebook
- Twitter
- School Websites (Google Sites)
- Microsoft Teams
- YouTube

References

Bass, B. (1997). Does the transactional – Transformational leadership paradigm transcend organizational and national boundaries? *American Psychology, 52*(2), 130–139.

Camburn, E. (2003). Distributive leadership in schools: The case of elementary schools adopting comprehensive school reform models. *Educational Evaluation and Policy Analysis, 25*(4).

Conventions on the Rights of the Child. (2021). Retrieved from https://www.ohchr .org/en/professionalinterest/pages/crc.aspx.

Deluga, R. (1990). The effects of transformational, transactional, and Laissez-Faire leadership characteristics on subordinate influencing behavior. *Basic and Applied Social Psychology, 11*(2), 191–203.

Developmentally Appropriate Practice (DAP) Position Statement. (2021). Retrieved from https://www.naeyc.org/resources/position-statements/dap/contents.

Erikson, E. (1963). *Childhood and society* (2nd ed.). New York: Norton.

Frey, N., Fisher, D., & Smith, D. (2019). *All learning is social and emotional: Helping students develop essential skills for the classroom and beyond*. Alexandria, VA: ASCD.

Fundamentals of sel. CASEL. (2022, March 11). Retrieved April 20, 2022, from https://casel.org/fundamentals-of-sel/

Gallegos, D., Eivers, A., Sondergeld, P., & Pattinson, C. (2021). Food insecurity and child development: A state-of-the-art review. *International Journal of Environmental Research and Public Health, 18*(17) 8990.

Gardner, H. (1983). *Multiple intelligences: The theory in practice*. New York: Basic Bs.

Gronlu. (20 ~upport children's approaches to learning? Play with them! Nr.. . Retrieved ho.. //www.naeyc.org/our-work/families/support -learning-with-play

Hattie, J. (2008). *Visible learning* (1st ed.). London: Routledge.

Howard, M. (2009). *RTI from all sides: What every teacher needs to know*. Portsmouth, NH: Heinemann.

Howell, J., & Avolio, B. (1993). Transformational leadership, transactional leadership, locus of control, and support for innovation: Key predictors of consolidated-business-unit performance. *Journal of Applied Psychology, 78*(6), 891–902.

Intelligence. (2021). In dictionary.cambridge.org. Retrieved June 13, 2021, from https://dictionary.cambridge.org/dictionary/english/intelligence.

International Literacy Association. (2018). *Children's rights to read.* Retrieved from www.literacyworldwide.org.

Jenkins, B. (2009). What it takes to be an instructional leader. National Association for Elementary School Principals 34–37. Retrieved from https://www.naesp.org/sites/default/files/J-F_p34.pdf.

Klar, H. W. (2012). Fostering distributed instructional leadership: A sociocultural perspective of leadership development in urban high schools. *Leadership and Policy in Schools*, 11(14) 365–390.

Kunz, K., Hall, M., & Lella, R. (2020). *Literacy changemakers: Bringing the joy of reading and writing into focus for teachers and students.* New York: Guilford Press.

Leithwood, K., Menzies, T., Jantzi, D., & Leithwood, J. (1996). School restructuring, transformational leadership and the amelioration of teacher burnout. *Anxiety, Stress and Coping: An International Journal, 9*(3), 199–215.

Louden, W., & Rohl, M. (2008). *Classroom literacy observation schedule - revised (CLOS-R).* Perth: The University of Western Australia.

Mendez, E. (2021). Smart growth for new school leaders. Edutopia. George Lucas Educational Foundation.

Mitgang, L., Gill, J., & Cummings, H. J. (2013). Districts matter: Cultivating the principals urban schools need. T. W. Foundation, Producer, & The Wallace Foundation.

Morrow, L. (2020). *Literacy development in the early years: Helping children read and write* (9th ed.). London: Pearson.

National Association for the Education of Young Children. (2021). Retrieved from https://www.naeyc.org/.

Noddings, N. (2013). *Caring: A relational approach to ethics and moral education.* Berkeley, CA: University of California Press.

Parkay, F., Anctil, E., & Hass, G. (2014). *Curriculum leadership: Readings for developing quality educational programs.* Englewood Cliffs, NJ: Prentice Hall.

Piaget, J. (1926). *The language and thought of the child.* New York: Harcourt Brace.

Sara Horton-Deutsch, P. C. (2013, February). Thinking it through: The path to reflective leadership. *American Nurse Today, 8*(2).Retrieved from https://www.myamericannurse.com/thinking-it-through-the-path-to-reflective-leadership/

Schunk, D. (2020). *Learning theories: An educational perspective* (8th ed.). London: Pearson.

Strike, K. (2006). *Ethical leadership in schools.* Retrieved from https://www.perlego.com/book/1005568/ethical-leadership-in-schools-pdf (Original work published 2006)